Al-Anon's Twelve Steps & Twelve Traditions

Al-Anon books and their ISBN listings:

Alateen: Hope for Children of Alcoholics
0-910034-20-6

The Dilemma of the Alcoholic Marriage
0-910034-18-4

Al-Anon Family Groups
0-910034-54-0

One Day at a Time in Al-Anon
0-910034-21-4
0-910034-63-X *Large Print*

Lois Remembers
0-910034-23-0

Alateen: A Day at a Time
0-910034-53-2

As We Understood. . .
0-910034-56-7

...In All Our Affairs: Making Crises Work for You
0-910034-73-7

Courage to Change: One Day at a Time in Al-Anon II
0-910034-79-6
0-910034-84-2 *Large Print*

From Survival to Recovery: Growing Up in an Alcoholic Home
0-910034-97-4

Courage To Be Me--Living with Alcoholism
0-910034-30-3

How Al-Anon Works for Families and Friends of Alcoholics
0-910034-26-5

Paths to Recovery - Al-Anon's Steps, Traditions and Concepts
0-910034-31-1

Having Had a Spiritual Awakening...
0-910034-33-8

Al-Anon's Twelve Steps & Twelve Traditions

AL-ANON FAMILY GROUP HEADQUARTERS, INC.
World Service Office for Al-Anon and Alateen
Virginia Beach, Virginia

For information and catalog of literature write to
World Service Office for Al-Anon and Alateen:
Al-Anon Family Group Headquarters, Inc.
1600 Corporate Landing Parkway
Virginia Beach, VA 23454-5617
Phone: (757) 563-1600   Fax: (757) 563-1655

This book is also available in: Danish, Finnish, French, German, Hebrew,
Italian, Norwegian, Polish, Portuguese, Spanish, and Swedish.

Al-Anon/Alateen is supported by member's voluntary contributions and
from the sale of our Conference Approved Literature.

Library of Congress Catalog Card No. 83-28087
ISBN-0-910034-24-9

Publisher's Cataloging in Publication

Al-Anon's twelve steps &twelve traditions.
  p. cm.
  Includes index.
  LCCN 83-028087.
  ISBN 0-910034-24-9

  1. Alcoholics— Family relationships. 2. Alcoholics—Rehabilitation.
3. Al-Anon Family Group Headquarters,inc. 4. Alcoholics Anonymous.
I.Al-Anon Family Group Headquarters, inc. II. Title: Al-Anon's twelve
steps and twelve traditions.

HV5278.A66 1990   362.292'3
                                     QBI92-20146

Approved by
World Service Conference
Al-Anon Family Groups

19-15M-99-7.50   B-8   Printed in U.S.A.

The Al-Anon Family Groups are a fellowship of relatives and friends of alcoholics who share their experience, strength and hope in order to solve their common problems. We believe alcoholism is a family illness and that changed attitudes can aid recovery.

Al-Anon is not allied with any sect, denomination, political entity, organization or institution; does not engage in any controversy, neither endorses nor opposes any cause. There are no dues for membership. Al-Anon is self-supporting through its own voluntary contributions.

Al-Anon has but one purpose: to help families of alcoholics. We do this by practicing the Twelve Steps, by welcoming and giving comfort to families of alcoholics, and by giving understanding and encouragement to the alcoholic.

The Suggested Preamble to the Twelve Steps

The Serenity Prayer

God grant me the serenity
To accept the things I cannot change,
Courage to change the things I can,
And wisdom to know the difference.

CONTENTS

Part II — The Twelve Traditions

PREFACE

Al-Anon's Twelve Steps and Twelve Traditions are for people whose lives have been, or are being, affected by the alcoholism of a spouse, parent, child, other relative, or friend. The foundation of our program, these twenty-four statements have served us well by keeping us centered on our own purpose, independent of all other procedures, therapies and organizations.

The Twelve Steps of Al-Anon are the heart of the program in which the family of an alcoholic can find a new way of life in the fellowship of the Al-Anon Family Groups. The Twelve Traditions are the backbone of Al-Anon itself. They guard the unity of the fellowship on which individual help depends.

The Twelve Steps and Traditions, although spiritually oriented, are not based on a specific religious discipline. They embrace not only the philosophies of the Judeo-Christian faiths and the many religions of the East, but non-religious, ethical and moral thought as well; nor does the designation "God" refer to a particular being, force or concept, but only to God as each of us understands that term. And so, those who do not subscribe to a particular faith can still find in this program a serene, fulfilling way of life, if they can believe in any Power greater than themselves.

In the years these Steps and Traditions have been studied and applied by the members of our fellowship, many among us discovered these guides had a far wider usefulness than in coping with alcoholism problems alone. They became our way of life, to help us at all times, in any situation. How well they served us depended on how we absorbed them, and how we used them. We have shared these experiences in this book and followed with one reflection and a story for each Step and Tradition. These are merely examples; there are as many stories as there are Al-Anon members.

INTRODUCTION

It all began with the wives of early AA members who realized their own need for change. They came together while their husbands were at meetings, and as they waited, talked over their own difficulties and tried to help each other find solutions. In helping each other, they tried to apply AA's Twelve Steps to their own lives, each group making whatever changes it felt was necessary.

By 1948, some 87 groups and individuals had asked AA for listing in its directory. These requests were referred to Lois, the wife of AA's co-founder, who became the co-founder of the Al-Anon Family Groups. Lois and her friends set about unifying these groups and providing them with guidance and service.

It was soon apparent that there would have to be a program with which all groups were in agreement. The adaptation of AA's Steps in final form came about after a number of these scattered groups had been brought together as a unified fellowship under the name of "Al-Anon Family Groups." Thus, Al-Anon was born of a real need for sharing.

Although we were far too young and inexperienced as a fellowship to have established any Traditions of our own, we knew our unity depended upon living by some such guideline. Then the AA Traditions, also amended to fit the needs of Al-Anon, became part of the program.

In the early years, the only source of help for children affected by the drinking of others was to attend Al-Anon and AA meetings. It was at these meetings with their parents that they learned about alcoholism and its effects on the family.

In 1957, a high school boy in California felt the need to talk with others who could identify with his sharing. Out of this need, other Al-Anon Family Groups were created and called "Alateen." As an integral part of Al-Anon, Alateen members follow the same program.

Al-Anon's Twelve Steps & Twelve Traditions

Part I

THE TWELVE STEPS

THE SUGGESTED PREAMBLE
TO THE TWELVE STEPS

The Al-Anon Family Groups are a fellowship of relatives and friends of alcoholics who share their experience, strength and hope in order to solve their common problems. We believe alcoholism is a family illness and that changed attitudes can aid recovery.

Al-Anon is not allied with any sect, denomination, political entity, organization or institution; does not engage in any controversy, neither endorses nor opposes any cause. There are no dues for membership. Al-Anon is self-supporting through its own voluntary contributions.

Al-Anon has but one purpose: to help families of alcoholics. We do this by practicing the Twelve Steps, by welcoming and giving comfort to families of alcoholics, and by giving understanding and encouragement to the alcoholic.

THE TWELVE STEPS

1. We admitted we were powerless over alcohol—that our lives had become unmanageable.
2. Came to believe that a Power greater than ourselves could restore us to sanity.
3. Made a decision to turn our will and our lives over to the care of God *as we understood Him.*
4. Made a searching and fearless moral inventory of ourselves.
5. Admitted to God, to ourselves and to another human being the exact nature of our wrongs.
6. Were entirely ready to have God remove all these defects of character.
7. Humbly asked Him to remove our shortcomings.
8. Made a list of all persons we had harmed, and became willing to make amends to them all.
9. Made direct amends to such people wherever possible, except when to do so would injure them or others.
10. Continued to take personal inventory and when we were wrong promptly admitted it.
11. Sought through prayer and meditation to improve our conscious contact with God *as we understood Him,* praying only for knowledge of His will for us and the power to carry that out.
12. Having had a spiritual awakening as the result of these Steps, we tried to carry this message to others, and to practice these principles in all our affairs.

THE STEPS
AND
THEIR STRUCTURE

As we study and apply the Twelve Steps, we see more and more clearly how carefully they were thought out, and the skill and precision with which each word was chosen. Written in the past tense, they share the experiences of those who have gone before us and offer us an ongoing guide for recovery today.

The first three Steps suggest that our human resources, such as intelligence, knowledge, strength, and even hope, are not enough to solve our problems. As others have done, we need to accept the help of a Power greater than our own to guide our thoughts and actions. These three Steps show us how to bring that Power into our lives in an active, workable partnership.

Step Four suggests the first action to be taken. This is reinforced by Steps Five, Six and Seven which point the way to overcome the personal faults that have caused so many of our problems.

Step Eight and Nine are again action Steps. They ask us to make specific corrections to relieve us of our burdens of guilt and confusion. Step Ten asks us to continue the effort begun with Step Four: searching out our shortcomings and working constantly to rid ourselves of them.

Step Eleven urges us to establish a conscious contact with a Power greater than ourselves through prayer and meditation; Step Twelve suggests the need to practice these principles in all our affairs, and to share our spiritual growth with others.

STEP ONE

We admitted we were powerless over alcohol—that
our lives had become unmanageable.

Many of us came to Al-Anon to learn the "secret" of compelling
a well-loved someone to stop the damaging and degrading over-
use of alcohol. How discouraging it seemed at first to be told there
was nothing we could do to force anyone to seek sobriety. Helpless
and hopeless, we were still not ready to surrender. Yet, how
encouraging it was to learn that we were not responsible for the
drinking, as so many of us feared we were.

By taking Step One we acknowledged that we had no power to
make another person stop drinking; that threats, pleas and the
determined use of our will were equally futile. Our schemes and
threats had succeeded only in our being physically and emotionally
exhausted. We were powerless; we were asked to admit that and
believe it if we wanted to make progress in improving the quality
of our lives.

Others of us, who had shouldered major responsibilities, may
have found it difficult to let go and to admit we were powerless
over something in our lives that we felt must be changed. We
thought of it as defeat and were determined not to be defeated in
what we considered a worthy goal, the sobriety of a family member or friend.

Some of us, when we first turned to Al-Anon for help, were in
no frame of mind to admit anything but how badly life was treat-

ing us. How difficult it was for us to face the idea that there was an area in which we were so helpless. By going to Al-Anon meetings and talking to other members, we reminded ourselves of this day by day. It became easier to accept something we knew we could not master. Learning that alcoholism was a disease proved to be a great relief. We realized that arguments were useless against a disease. We concluded that nothing we could do directly would stop an alcoholic's drinking or change another person.

At the same time, there were those of us who came to our first Al-Anon meetings after our loved ones had stopped drinking. In the first glow of sobriety some were unrealistically certain our lives would now be perfect. For others there were new fears and resentments as the alcoholic sought his or her solutions without us. We too had to realize the futility of trying to control. When we found ourselves continuing to direct, we reminded ourselves that we had no power, no right to exercise power, over anyone but ourselves.

Once we accepted these facts, we discovered an important and inspiring secret: how to free ourselves from frustration and confusion and set ourselves on the way to becoming contented, well-adjusted people.

When our eyes and ears and hearts were opened, we could free ourselves from our rigid determination to have things the way we wanted them. Then we began to grow.

We began this growth when we overcame the impulse to criticize or blame when we thought we had reason to do so; we reminded ourselves that we would probably only be making matters worse.

The feelings of release, of yielding or letting go, when we acknowledged that no change in others can be forced, helped to loosen the suffocating grip of our destructive emotions: guilt, fear, self-pity, resentment. We found, to our surprise, a new feeling of relaxation, as though a weight of care had been lifted from us. In Al-Anon, we express our emotional detachment from our problems in such sayings as "Live and Let Live" and "Let Go and Let God."

Freed from the obsession with another person, we could focus our attention on ourselves. We looked at how our lives had become unmanageable. How did we change our negative attitudes? How did we find the path to self-awareness? What actions did we take to change ourselves for the better and how and where did we get the help we needed?

Our answers lay in taking the Twelve suggested Steps toward recovery which had been used successfully by others with the same problems. We began with the cornerstone of them all—Step One.

Some order came out of chaos. It became easier and easier to accept the idea we could take charge of ourselves. Each time we detached we moved forward.

With our admissions that we lacked power over alcohol, that we lacked the ability to direct other people's lives, that our lives were unmanageable, we were ready to look beyond ourselves for the strength we needed to live a new way of life.

Thinking It Over

It isn't easy to admit defeat, especially when I tried for so long to handle my problems in my own way. But I do know that I cannot move forward unless I am willing to stop trying to control others and their compulsions. From my friends in the program, I can reinforce my knowledge of the futility of struggling against another person's drinking or thinking.

I know that those who come in contact with the family disease are affected in their actions and reactions, but I was the one who allowed my life to become troubled and confused, my thinking so warped. If I can take my eyes off others, I can see those things in me which contributed to the harshness of my life. I can remind myself that progress in my recovery from all the anger and frustration can only begin with what I can bring myself to do. I can only begin my search for serenity when I can free myself from my obsession with others.

A Step-One Story

My husband Pete left on a Friday morning to go into the city to be interviewed for still another job. At my urgent pleading, he promised faithfully to be home by evening.

I should have known! Another sleepless night, watching at the window, wondering what had happened this time. How could I have believed in him when he said he'd be back? No use checking the local bars, I thought to myself, the way I usually did; he was surely still in the city.

I had promised our local liquor store man that I'd be around on Saturday morning to cover one of Pete's bounced checks. That happened so often, and every time they called me to take care of it, I did. I started out with a heavy heart.

On the way from our house to the nearby railroad station, there's a six-lane highway. Just as I was about to cross, the light turned red, and to my horror, there was Pete on the other side, trying to stagger into all that traffic. My first impulse was to rush over, but I knew how hopeless that would be. In my utter desperation, I closed my eyes and said, "Oh, God! Oh, God!"

When I heard the traffic stop for the changing light, I looked up and there, across the highway, was a stalwart stranger with a firm grip on my husband's arm, steering him safely over. When they got to me, I thanked the man, with my voice shaking.

It was then I realized that this life-and-death crisis had been taken care of—and not by me. I was powerless, but God was not. It was then that I finally understood the meaning of the First Step.

There was still that check to take care of; I had promised. But I swore that this would be the last time and I meant it. I went into the liquor store, still trembling from that shocking experience. I explained that I would cover no more of Pete's checks; if he was willing to give him credit, he'd have to collect from Pete. The man agreed, and then said, "You know, that husband of yours ought to try AA."

What irony! I told him how I'd been trying for years to get him to go.

"Well," he answered, "maybe you've been trying too hard."

After that day I found a new direction. I was free. That one unforgettable shock had brought me to my senses and showed me that I was actually prolonging the problem by trying to run everything. From then on, it was "hands off."

That decision brought about many changes in our lives, because I had learned the true and total purpose of that First Step. My life had become completely chaotic and unmanageable—until I learned of my own little bit of power.

STEP TWO

Came to believe that a Power greater than ourselves could restore us to sanity.

Taking Step One brought us face-to-face with the truth: We were not equal to the task of changing any other human being. We needed more than our human experience and intelligence to solve the problems of living, especially of living with an alcoholic, whether still drinking or not.

Taking the Second Step suggests that we were not alone with those problems, if we "came to believe" that help was within our reach. The words "came to believe" meant a gradual awakening to the reality of a Higher Power in our lives. This Step brought us a glimmer of hope as we made our first timid moves toward establishing a working relationship with "a Power greater than ourselves." We began to perceive that this Power was ready to help us whenever we were ready to accept its guidance.

What could this Power do for us? It "could restore us to sanity."

This may have come as a shock to those of us who had always imagined it was only the alcoholic who needed to be restored to sanity. The very idea that one might not be sane usually brought heated denial. Whether spouse, parent, child or friend, many of us came to Al-Anon convinced that all the insanity belonged exclusively to the alcoholic. We were dismayed to learn that we, too, needed to change, that Al-Anon's program was centered on us, the friends and family who had been trying so hard to make some sense out of living, or having lived with an alcoholic.

To admit that we were irrational may have required more humility than most of us were blessed with. Yet, when we finally faced the fact that it was we who must change, or live with continued confusion and unhappiness, we found ourselves better able to accept the idea that humility was a vital tool in getting the healing help we needed; this Step foreshadows the entire spiritual scope of the Al-Anon program.

When we looked closely at ourselves and recalled what we were apt to say and do in this, or that, situation, we discovered that our behavior was often distorted by anger, frustration and fear. That is why many of us reacted to the alcoholic in irrational, hysterical ways. In other words, our actions had not been sane. It would have been only natural for us to think of self-justifying ways to defend what we did, but many learned that our actions were indefensible.

Irrational behavior takes many forms. What about the husband who leaves young children with a drinking wife and worries himself sick over what might happen while he is away at work? Or a wife who is so scared of her violent husband that she does nothing to protect herself or her children from his unpredictable behavior? Or one who would allow a child to get into an automobile with a drinking or drunken parent at the wheel?

Consider also the spouses or parents who do everything they can to protect alcoholic loved ones from the consequences of drinking. They hide the addiction from relatives and friends, lie for them to employers, plead with judges and even try to carry the drinker to a comfortable bed so he, or she, won't have to face having passed out on the floor the night before! Some people are even so confused they think drinking with the alcoholic will leave that much less for them to drink!

Sometimes, actions of this kind were motivated by good intentions; more often, by rage and disappointment. But there was almost always an underlying idea that something just might make the alcoholic stop drinking. All we had to do, we imagined, was to figure what that "something" was. Even that attitude was far from sane, we learned. Upon reflection, we decided whether our thoughts, words and actions were those of well-balanced, reasonable people. If we realized they were not, then we needed help, the kind of spiritual help to be found in Al-Anon.

Once we learned to see our situation as it really was, we understood why it was necessary for us to turn to a Power greater than ourselves. At that point in our Al-Anon experience, it might have been too soon to expect total trust in a Higher Power, especially, since we thought we were self-reliant. At one time, we might have believed in God, but never called on Him except in conventional prayers; we might have thought of Him only as a malevolent demon punishing us for we knew not what. Those of us who were brought up in a religious faith may have naturally used prayer to ask God for what we wanted. Surely, most of us prayed for something to change the drinker into a normal, responsible human being.

The non-believers admitted to being powerless to control all the events of their lives, but with the help and support of Al-Anon, trust in a "Power greater than ourselves" came in time. That meant being allied to an unfailing source of security and comfort.

That is not to say we didn't have setbacks and disappointments, but we learned to see these as stages in our growth, opportunities to learn something we needed to know. They gave us a new perspective and prepared us for solutions we couldn't have foreseen. Accepting disappointments, often unrelated to alcoholism, with calm poise, saved wear and tear on the nerves, as well as demonstrating our confidence that things ultimately worked out as they were meant to. This was by no means weak resignation, but intelligent recognition of the fact that life had experiences for us, some welcome, some not, but all of them offering insights.

It often happened that a newcomer, deep in despair, came to Al-Anon already determined to make a radical change in his, or her life, e.g., court action, separation or divorce. Al-Anon members who had been at this crossroad themselves shared their experience and pointed out that there might be other options available. They know that Al-Anon members never advised another to take, or not to take action; particularly newcomers, who had not yet absorbed enough of the Al-Anon ideas to know they had other choices. We found that if we gave a member advice about what action to take, we were making unwarranted judgements and decisions that affected the lives of others. We could, however, share our own experiences and offer a measure of objectivity. Our detachment often lead others to make reasoned decisions, rather than emotional ones. In helping ourselves, we helped others to be restored to sanity; then they were better able to make their own decisions.

Thinking It Over

Perhaps, having thought over this Second Step, I can now say to myself: If I declare that "I came to believe," it means my thinking is already moving forward from Step One, in which I had to admit I was powerless.

I have also come to believe there is a way for me to bring order into my confused life. These Steps will help me, as I move on from one to the next.

Now here in Step Two, I am acknowledging there is a Power greater than I am. I know that my human will and wisdom work in the dark; there is so much I do not know about myself, or about others, even those who are close to me. There are things I may never know.

If my words and actions are prompted only by my own impulses, some of which may be negative, they can have troublesome consequences for me. When I have at last realized that my problems are too big to solve, by myself, then comes the bright, reassuring thought that I need not be alone with them, if I am willing to accept help from a Higher Power.

A Step-Two Story

For my first three years in Al-Anon, I had trouble with the Second Step. In spite of disclaimers in our literature and on the part of some members of the fellowship in the groups I attended, it seemed to me there was an effort to make me believe in a narrow religious interpretation of these Steps. I had not lost my belief in a Power greater than myself, but I came from a background of generations of dissenters from orthodoxy that began in England before the Pilgrims came to New England. I wondered, in order to become a good member of Al-Anon, was it necessary for me to believe in a God made in the image of man? (I'm a bearded male of advanced age and I knew this outward appearance did not make me in any way a counterpart of God.) Most of the time I kept my mouth shut, but I did a lot of troubled thinking about the theological implications of the Second Step. At a meeting, an older member said what I needed to hear to make me comfortable with the Steps in Al-Anon that mention a Higher Power or "God as I understood Him."

"Why worry about interpretations?" she said. "I have come to

believe that Al-Anon puts me in touch with the help I need to en-
able me to live a saner and more peaceful life. Why do I need to
trouble myself in trying to define the power that I know is there?
'We came to believe a Power greater than ourselves could restore
us to sanity.' As Dr. Bob, co-founder of AA, said shortly before he
died—'Let's not louse this up. Let's keep it simple.' She continued,
"The Steps are not commandments; they are a set of principles
that can bring about a spiritual awakening. They describe shared
experiences. As long as I share in these experiences, I don't need to
let words, and/or interpretations, get in my way."

Because it is so important for me to find my own way, I have also
tried to respect other people's beliefs or doubts. I simply try to
share my own strengths without trying to impose my beliefs on
others. We are all equals but we are not all the same.

STEP THREE

*Made a decision to turn our will and our lives over
to the care of God as we understood Him.*

Rarely has a complete pattern for living been compressed into so few words. It grows naturally out of Steps One and Two; first, we acknowledged that we had been unable to manage our lives; then, we accepted the idea that our help came from a Power greater than ourselves, and made a decision to place our lives in the care of that Power. It was, perhaps, the most important decision we ever made, carrying with it a compelling need to keep aware of it always. Once we had made that decision and kept reminding ourselves of it, our Higher Power became a part of our daily lives.

Accepting the Third Step was a discipline we set for ourselves. It took vigilance not to slip, and take back the reins into our own hands. We had been trying to solve our problems, make choices and determine our actions, by means of our fallible human wisdom and will power alone. It was not enough; our failures and disappointments proved this. When we made plans, we realized that we couldn't possibly take every contingency into account; this, too, explains why we were often frustrated by failure. We had many changes to make and we were able to begin by trying to learn how to use the help of a Higher Power.

Making this decision to put ourselves in the care of a Higher Power took courage, and above all, it took confidence. It served us well when, day after day, we kept alert to what we were thinking, saying, and doing. It helped to form the habit of including our Higher Power in our thoughts when we had a decision to make. When we thought of it as a daily, even hourly, undertaking, it was amazing how readily we acquired the habit.

Every time we consciously reminded ourselves of this Step, and followed through on it, we experienced a feeling of achievement and growth. Many a long-time Al-Anon member had the thrilling experience of seeing changes take place in newcomers, as they gradually shed their despair, and week-by-week, grew in confidence and understanding.

Then, we went for the next phrase of Step Three's wonderfully compact plan for living: "to turn our will and our lives over . . . " This will of ours grew out of our personality, experience and habits, which even the most earnest and determined could not change overnight. It was the quality that made us sure we were right. It tempted us to justify what we did and closed our minds to the possibility we might be mistaken. Without spiritual underpinnings, we found ourselves hard-pressed to overcome the drive of a strong will. Such a will, set on a fixed goal, could have the seed of defeat built right into it. It might have gotten what it was after, but in the end, this triumph would have turned to ashes of frustration.

All this applied, also, to the "turning over" of our lives. Day-by-day we functioned, more or less automatically; we dealt with the present moment, the current crisis, in the accustomed way, rarely stopping to think whether there was a better way. Yet, we like to think that we had control over our lives and we expected our decisions to turn out well. We have only to look back on our many disappointments to realize that our control was at best rare, and more often an illusion.

Now, where could we look for the help we expected when we "turned over our will and our lives?" Obviously there was no person, no address, we could go to for the answers we needed. This might have been our first realization that a benign Power was at hand, ready to guide us when we were ready to be guided. This was a spiritual gift, an opportunity to be helped, not only when we could not help ourselves, but even when we imagined we could. Our part in this relationship was to learn to recognize, reach out, accept—and act, with the inner awareness of the spiritual presence whose direction we decided to follow when we made a decision to turn over our will and our lives.

What did we have to lose by making this decision? Only our stubborn determination to have things our way; only the despair that came from repeated disappointments. And what did we gain? A new life, with purpose, meaning, and constant progress, and all the contentment and fulfillment that comes from such growth.

We came then to the closing words of this Third Step: ". . . as we understood Him." It was left entirely up to us what the name God meant to us, personally. We might have imagined Him to be a ruler and judge, dealing out rewards and punishments. Or the God of our understanding might have been the quality of Universal Love, revealing itself in our lives. To some it might have been a personal God, powerful, but separate from us, while to others, God might have been thought of as an essential part of all creativity.

God, as we understood Him, was not filtered through any group, not limited to any teaching, and our understanding grew as we developed spiritually through working with these Steps. The choice was and is ours alone. The opportunity to use Divine guidance is given to us all to interpret and use as we wish.

Thinking It Over

All the experience of my life, my patterns of thought and attitude, are so much a part of me that everything I think, say, and do has become an automatic reaction to what happens outside of me.

Step Three suggests I teach myself, from this moment on, to be receptive, to open myself to help from my Higher Power; a help which may come in many forms, often through other people. I will try to keep in mind that this relationship I have with God does not mean merely asking for His help, but knowing it is there and accepting it.

It's as though I were standing on the shore of a river, my children on the opposite side, hungry, cold and frightened. There is a boat at hand, with warm blankets, clothing and food. Would I just stand there, imploring God to save my children, when He has already provided everything I need? No, I'd get into the boat and row across, wrap up the children warmly, feed them and thank God for knowing my need.

So it is with other problems I may have. Until I have established a relationship with a Higher Power, I may miss many of the obvious solutions to my difficulties.

A Step-Three Story

Except for a rare visit to a nearby city, I had never been away from my home town. I married young, had six children, and then separated from my alcoholic husband. In Al-Anon, I was slow to grasp the program, but as each bit of it sank in, I grew in confidence.

My oldest daughter, nineteen, joined the Navy and was sent to a mid-western training station. Things seemed to be going pretty well with her, when suddenly I had a call from her training base, saying she was in the hospital because of an emotional breakdown. I nearly panicked, but I'd really learned to ask for guidance and that was the first thing I did. One thing I knew, I had to get to my child somehow. But how? I had no money. I'd never traveled and I didn't know how to go about getting around in new places. Again and again I almost lost touch with God. I forced myself to keep in mind that He would help me find the way.

I borrowed money for the plane to the nearest big city. From there I knew I'd find some way to get to the Navy base after I arrived. I called our Al-Anon group secretary and she rushed over with the Al-Anon World Directory. In it I found two names and telephone numbers of members I could call to tell me what kind of transportation to take to the base hospital.

When the plane landed, I had just one thought—make a contact with Al-Anon. The first person I called was Barbara. I told her my story and asked her how to get to the base. She told me where to get a bus to the nearest town where she'd be waiting for me.

I don't know how we recognized each other, but Barbara was there to meet me and drove me the ten miles to the base hospital. On the way, as we talked, she said: "You mentioned finding a place to stay. You won't need one. We have an extra room, and that will make it handy for driving you to the hospital to see your girl."

I was so overwhelmed that I cried. But I knew it wasn't just two strangers meeting, it was two Al-Anons, living with a Higher Power who had taken charge of this crisis.

My daughter was so relieved to see me that she soon showed signs of improvement. Barbara drove me over there every day for a week, and made me feel altogether at home. Every time I spoke of how grateful I was to her, she'd say, "Don't you think this is doing just as much for me?"

She even drove me all the way back to my homebound plane, a distance of fifty-odd miles. And I went with a lightened heart, for the doctor had assured me that my daughter would soon be well enough to return to duty.

This, to me, was Step Three at work. I didn't know where I was going, how I'd get there, or where I'd stay, only that it was all in God's hands.

STEP FOUR

Made a searching and fearless moral inventory of ourselves.

Of the Twelve Steps, seven are action parts of the Al-Anon program. The process of our personal improvement began with Step Four in which we tackled the real spadework of getting to know ourselves as we really were.

Maybe we'd been so preoccupied with thinking about what others were up to, especially the alcoholic, that we never realized how much our own actions needed examining. It was inspiring to realize that we had the ability to become more confident, competent, and mature. Self-discovery was a satisfying goal to look forward to, well worth every bit of effort we put into it; but we tried to remember that this was not a singlehanded, personal effort—we asked for, and accepted the help of a Higher Power, every step of the way. We simply could not work alone.

Step Four was a tool for bringing to light the true source of our problems. As we dug deeper to discover just how our own shortcomings had frustrated us, we began to see what needed to be changed, in us, not in anybody else. We learned gradually how many of our difficulties were of our own making, and could not be blamed on fate, bad luck, or the selfishness and stubbornness of other people.

We took an *inventory*. That's a word usually applied to tangible things: so many chairs, coats, rugs, money and other possessions.

25

That kind of inventory is easy enough; those are things we could see and touch. The Step-Four Inventory, however, was made up of our personal characteristics, as we understood and evaluated them. That evaluation, naturally, was colored by our attitudes, our personal experience and how honest we could be in recognizing them.

All of us had qualities, some we liked, some we didn't and some we were not even aware of; and our good qualities gave us strong support in correcting the ones that gave us trouble. We may have been tempted to excuse some of our faults because we felt others had treated us badly. Some we may have justified because we felt "Everybody does that." We may have had an irresistible drive to control a situation and those involved in it. But the sole purpose of the "searching and fearless inventory" was to shed light on what was standing in the way of achieving fulfillment.

We began the process of improving as soon as we uncovered the various personal qualities that made us the way we were. Above all, we needed to get a clear picture of our attitudes and actions toward others—our family members, our relatives, friends, co-workers. It wasn't easy. Long-established habits were hard to recognize and even harder to change. Many people in Al-Anon admit that Step Four was a challenge almost too formidable to face. It was easier to hide and continue to deny the unpleasant and painful truths. This is understandable; it isn't easy to evaluate deep-rooted attitudes and habits. Many found it helpful to do a written inventory, others wrote their life story. When we recorded significant events in our lives and honestly wrote how we felt about them, we discovered that our defects were not caused by having lived with an alcoholic; we already had human imperfections which would have caused us trouble under any circumstances.

It was important not to condemn ourselves for whatever negative qualities we uncovered in this self-study. Most of us were already burdened with feelings of guilt. Many of us wondered uneasily whether we might have been responsible for the alcoholic's drinking, before we learned in Al-Anon that alcoholism is a disease we could not have prevented. Blaming ourselves for mistakes we made was not a productive way to improvement.

A great lift came as we realized that we were not alone in this undertaking. The guidance and support of our Higher Power was always at hand, reinforced by understanding and loving friends in the Al-Anon group. it was only our own improvement we were striving for, our own flaws we wanted to get rid of. Measuring our shortcomings by comparing them to those of others only hampered our search for self-understanding. Thus a searching and fearless inventory meant no side-stepping. The inventory in which we listed our character flaws was only a starting point. The main advantage of such a list was that it showed us how to contrast our undesirable characteristics with the good ones that offset them.

Recognizing and acknowledging some of our shortcomings wasn't easy; these were the very ones which most needed to be rooted out. Then too, it was to be a "moral" inventory, one directly relating to, or dealing with the distinction between right and wrong in our conduct. Because each of us had developed our own code of ethics, we took this into account in making our own "moral" inventories. We examined our behavior as it affected us, other people in our lives, and especially those close to us.

Thinking It Over

As I see it, my own shortcomings may be due to confusion, fear or uneasiness. When I find I am impatient and unreasonable, it is per-

*haps because I have taken on more than I can handle. I'm under
such pressure that I can't even recognize how badly I'm reacting.
Looking for the causes, I find, first, I have too much to do in a given
time period. Maybe I've allowed thoughtless friends to interrupt my
work, or I may have been faced with a dreaded obligation or faced
with a dilemma to be solved. Once I determined the cause, I can set
about getting rid of my impatience and unreasonableness.*

*In the same way, I can ultimately cope with self-righteousness and
intolerance. Perhaps I'm afraid to accept ideas other than those I
have lived with for so long. It may be hard for me to see social and
political changes without feeling that "the old ways were better."
When self-pity rears its ugly head, I know I am overlooking the
many blessings in my life for which I should be grateful.*

*Surely I can work out the causes of the flaws I acknowledge in my
list. I am determined to concentrate on the reasons why I act the way
I do in various situations, and then try to eliminate the underlying
causes.*

*I know it will be a big help for me to cultivate awareness of people.
I can listen to what they are saying, observe their actions accept them
and try to understand.*

A Step-Four Story

Since my husband, Don, made a decision to live without alcohol, we have been able to discuss our problems free of the distorting cloud of active alcoholism.

A remark he made gave me the first inkling of how inconsistent
my behavior had become. He said that when I was happy I didn't
worry so much about my gardening. That made me think.

I went to bed with this on my mind, and when I woke up, the

thought was still there. Half-awake, I let my mind explore my obsession with gardening as it must have appeared to Don.

For many years, I made plants my hobby—if it grew, I had to have it. Finding room for them all was my major concern. I denied us the convenience of a larger apartment so I wouldn't have to give up my backyard. I cut short our vacations because my plants needed care; I spent my week-ends rearranging, repotting and watering my plants, even working harder than I do during the week at my job. I had been rewarded with much beauty—but, I had allowed it to become an obsession. Not verbally, but my manner showed I had expected my husband to share my hobby. If I could not get at my gardening, I was as strained and unhappy as the alcoholic when he couldn't get a drink! I was living in a prison of my own making. We couldn't use our barbecue because every table and chair in the yard was covered with plants. It was the same indoors; Don had to move several plants before he could draw the shower curtain. He couldn't close the blinds in our room because the plants needed light. The heat in the living room was regulated to keep the plants healthy.

As obsessions go, my plants were among the least harmful, but I was determined to break the habit of being a slave to them and making them dominate our lives. Life has been far happier since I made that discovery and did something about it.

STEP FIVE

Admitted to God, to ourselves and to another human being the exact nature of our wrongs.

Humility is the underlying thought of the Twelve Steps. The pattern was set for us by Step One: "admitted we were powerless." In Step Two we acknowledged a Power greater than ourselves; in Step Three, we relinquished control by deciding to "turn our will and our lives over" to that Power. In Step Four we faced up to our shortcomings. All this is concerned with the quality and purpose of *humility*.

The Step before this one started us on a continuing process of uncovering what we were really like. We learned day by day, to observe what actions might have kept us from realizing our true potential, and getting from life the serenity it could bring. We decided to do a three-fold "admitting": to God, to ourselves, and to another person.

Admitting to God—first—prepared us for the two things we had to do next: admit our shortcomings to ourselves and to another human being.

It was not a matter of informing our Higher Power of something only we knew. It was rather the effect on *us* of feeling that we could, in a sense, speak to our God without embarrassment or shame. This provided us with a solid base for a clear understanding of ourselves. It was this intimate communication with a Higher Power that made us feel all the more free to bring out everything

31

that needed to come to light. In consciously telling God, we en-
lightened ourselves about the ways in which we wanted to change.

Our method of communicating with God depended on our personal view and our relationship to Him. Some of us might "speak"
to Him in thought, perhaps visualizing Him as a kind, understanding presence, or as an impersonal Universal Spirit. No matter how we chose to communicate with God, it was essential for us
to experience the feeling of surrender of our will. Then we would
have prepared ourselves for unquestioning acceptance of this
guidance in the days and years to come.

Step Five next asked us to admit our shortcomings to ourselves.
This might not have been easy, even after we had opened our
hearts to a spiritual power. It was helpful to check our Step-Four
list for such character flaws as arrogance, self-justification and resentment, for these three traits may have concealed other faults.
Strict honesty and courage had helped us with this added effort.
We might not have liked what we found, but once we had admitted our imperfections to ourselves, the improving process began.

We might have been tempted to justify our hostile or indifferent
feelings about others or to overlook whatever we found too painful to admit, but such evading would have surely hindered our
progress. If we were really trying to isolate our major faults, we
found it helpful to observe them in the way we reacted to the people in our daily lives. Such awareness could give us a clearer understanding of the causes of our failures and frustrations.

It was a good idea to undertake these self-examinations when
we had been annoyed or hurt by what somebody else had done.
We may have wondered why things worked out the way they did,
only to find it was our own attitude or action that created the unwelcome result. Even when we were not at fault, we learned about

ourselves when we became aware of our reactions and discovered what sort of situations had the power to hurt us.

When we reviewed the list of faults we made for Step Four, we found each of these related to some habit, some way we thought, acted, worked or spoke. If we were quick to resent, to imagine that others were purposely hurtful, we might have uncovered the reasons behind these thoughts by recalling actual instances in which this resentment made problems for us. If our resentment was due to unfulfilled expectations, then we needed to learn not to expect others to behave exactly as we wanted them to. If we resented what we regarded as a deliberate unkindness, we asked ourselves whom we were really hurting by feeling bitter. We realized, then, we were hurting only ourselves and not the person against whom we held a resentment.

The same thinking-through could be applied to other flaws we discovered. As we learned to understand why we reacted the way we did, we were ready for the next part of the Step and we shared the nature of our shortcomings with a friend.

Choosing a helpful, understanding Al-Anon member, someone who was really living the program, was a good idea. Usually, we did not choose a family member or a close relative—or the alcoholic. Before we decided on confiding in a member of the clergy, we took into account that trustworthiness was not the sole consideration. It was also important for our confidant to have knowledge of the program and the purpose of this Step.

Once we had decided on a dependable person, we tried to make our communication as open and honest as possible. There was much more to this than just presenting a list of our shortcomings; frank and detailed explanations were needed; how we felt about these faults, instances of how others responded to what we did, and so on. We found this telling and explaining far more natural and easy, if we were able to avoid feelings of guilt. After all, the faults we described were those we were not even aware of before we began our effort at self-improvement. We tried to refrain from passing judgment, even on ourselves.

In bringing our hidden thoughts about ourselves to another person, we were also asking for more than just to be heard. We ourselves were ready to listen to the other person's response to what we had told them. Their experience might not have been the same as ours; the interchange could only be productive and helpful if we were willing to listen with an open mind to someone else's view. We were broadened by accepting ideas that could change us for the better.

No matter how difficult we found this part of Step Five, it brought a tremendous sense of relief. It lightened our own burden to share it with another for whom it was not a burden, but an opportunity to help.

Thinking It Over

It is very comforting to know I can have a personal relationship with a Higher Power of my own choosing. Because God and I have an understanding, I am free to bring my shortcomings to this Spiritual Friend.

When I admit my imperfections to myself, I give myself a chance to make room for new attitudes and directions. My willingness to look beyond my defensive view, or my real or imagined hurts, gives me release from the job of carrying them around. If I can search them out and look at them, I can put them down.

Learning to trust and confide in another person means ridding myself of the prejudices I'd acquired with the disease of alcoholism. I can receive a special bonus in establishing this kind of rapport with an Al-Anon sponsor, who is able to share the recovery tools of the program when I share my feelings. I can use what I have learned to sponsor others. My sponsor listened, just listened. What relief it gave me to unburden myself and what a sense of freedom I felt. I will try to share my experiences without suggesting solutions for others.

A Step-Five Story

Some years ago, when I took myself through the Twelve Steps for the first time, I ran into quite a few problems with the middle Steps: Four, Five and Six. It wasn't until I reached Step Five that I began to uncover some of my most negative characteristics, although I hadn't realized what they were doing to me.

Sure, I'd made a list, as Step Four had told me to. It was as honest as I could make it, but even so, it wasn't much of a list. One of the shortcomings I admitted to was procrastination. I just couldn't seem to get things done that needed doing. I had several excuses; I had too much to do, I had been interrupted by others, or the days just weren't long enough. It didn't dawn on me that I was too busy minding other people's business, too busy taking charge of everything and everybody in the family, to take charge of myself.

That's how it went with my whole inventory. I'd put down a flaw and then immediately excuse it. Everything that was wrong with me seemed to be caused by the way other people failed to live up to what I expected of them. I felt pretty good about myself when I'd finished Step Four. It seemed to prove what I'd always known—that life had dealt me a pretty bad hand! Poor me! Seems

I forgot to include self-pity on my list. I just couldn't see that my own attitude had anything to do with my frustrations. So I marched confidently up to Step Five, certain that what I had to admit to God and to myself wasn't a half-bad record. But as for admitting to another person what was wrong with me, forget it! I didn't know anybody I trusted all that much and besides, I had no intention of laying myself open to criticism.

When that thought struck me, it brought me up short. It was like a sudden light in a dark room. Why was I so suspicious of other people? Why was I so afraid to see myself through someone else's eyes? Was that some kind of shortcoming in me? As these questions came springing into my mind, I began to have misgivings about how honest I'd been in my Fourth-Step inventory. And here was the Fifth, saying to me, "Watch what you're doing! Notice how you react to people. Listen to your own words—to the sound of your own voice. What makes you feel so sorry for yourself? Why don't you listen?"

I made up my mind to complete Step Five, the part I had shied away from, admitting to another human being what I'd found troublesome in me. I realized I couldn't handle this job all by myself, as I'd planned to do. That sudden insight, or inspiration, made me swallow my pride and decide to ask someone else to help me. But who? I suddenly realized I had hardly any friends, not even a close association with anyone in my group. It was a real problem but, as I was to learn, when I really needed help and admitted my need, help was at hand. I thought of my first sponsor in my early Al-Anon days who had been so patient with me. But after a few months in the program, I figured I knew more about it than anybody, so I gave up having a sponsor. Just the other day, when I was thinking back to that time, it dawned on me that I know less now, after six years in Al-Anon, than I thought I did then.

I called my sponsor, who was delighted to hear from me and agreed at once to work with me on the self-examination Steps.

It would take too long to tell you the many ways in which this helped straighten out my thinking. It took lots of patience and understanding, for I was a stubborn subject. But I could actually feel the changes taking place in me. I became willing, humbly willing, to turn to my Higher Power for help whenever I needed it. There was a growing confidence to be gained by dealing with my problems. And the way other people seemed to accept me, and even to like me—that was a revelation! And most important, my love for others kept growing and I could sense their acceptance and affection.

STEP SIX

Were entirely ready to have God remove all these defects of character.

The purpose of Step Six was to make ourselves ready to accept God's help and to know, with absolute certainty, when we had done so. Taking this Step continued to remind us that we needed the help of a Power greater than ourselves. This ever-available help, however, in no way relieved us of our responsibility to uncover and examine our defects.

We knew these defects might have their roots in deeply-ingrained patterns of behavior which were very much a part of us and could not be blamed on alcoholism. What was still harder to see and accept was that we were often as comfortable with these defects as with a pair of old shoes: The new self we were striving for may have pinched while we were adjusting to it, but only we could bring about changes that meant a new way of life. We could not forget we were dependent on a Power greater than ourselves if we really wanted to make a success of this undertaking. It was as though we were going on a journey to an unknown destination. We were eager to get there, but we could not find the way alone. So we reached out for the hand of the guide who pointed out the path we were to follow. But it was *we* who must do the traveling.

We may have imagined—maybe even with a feeling of hopelessness—that we were expected to achieve personal perfection. The Twelve Steps may seem to ask us to strive for a kind of impossible freedom from all faults. Not so! We came to believe their real purpose is to show us we have unlimited potential for solving the problems of living. They tell us we can remove the road-blocks—often self-created—that make it so laborious to achieve confidence and peace of mind. When we were first faced with a crisis, we may have examined it from all angles, desperately searching for a solution. We could see no way out, and we knew it was a problem nobody else could solve, but if we were able to open ourselves in total surrender to our Higher Power, the in-spiration that seemed to come from within us freed us from doubt and despair, providing secure confidence that the right answers would come. There, as at every Step, we realized how essential it was to refer all our problems, all our shortcomings, to that Higher Power.

When we clung to old habits and to unproductive ways of thinking, we blocked the process of change and the flow of inspi-ration. The sure way to use God's help was to allow solutions to come to us.

We might have wondered why we held on to our defects. Often they were developed as defenses—and they worked for us. Pride, for instance, allowed us to feel superior, indifferent to our common humanity and its responsibilities. Manipulating the lives of others gave us a feeling of being "in charge." As we learned to accept ourselves and love ourselves, the need for these defenses melted away.

Steps Four and Five helped us to uncover our defects of charac-ter. We have faced them courageously and shared them with another human being. We have acknowledged our shortcomings without guilt, or even regret, for we have learned that to blame and punish ourselves would not help us to grow. The guilt feelings were natural, but clinging to them kept us at a standstill.

We may have felt that this process of bringing about fundamental changes in ourselves was too demanding, even overwhelming. And so it might have been, but the fact that we turned to Al-Anon for help, that we faced the discipline of the Twelve Steps, implies a seriousness about wanting to tackle the troubles that make life so perplexing. Faith in our ability to follow through relieved us of anxiety and made it possible to face and solve, with spiritual wisdom, the problems of each day.

Were we then "entirely ready" to have our faults removed? Surely we would want a new image of ourselves. There is a radiant, confident personality in each of us, hidden under a welter of confusion, uncertainty and discontent. If someone were to ask if we wanted to be freed from these hindrances, there could be only one answer; that we were entirely ready to have God remove them.

Thinking It Over

I have decided I will not cling to the old, worn-out image of myself. I promise to carry in my thoughts the person I'd like to be. The way to do that is to keep alert to the ideas that come automatically to mind, consider the actions and words they suggest to me, and thus keep myself from acting on impulse.

A sudden spurt of temper can lead me to say hurtful things, often things I do not really mean. This accomplishes nothing—not for me nor for the person who sparked the irritation in me. Let me think before I speak, unless the impulse that prompts my words is courteous and loving.

Do I really want to continue criticizing and giving advice? Can I be sure my views are right? Has it ever occurred to me that I, too, do

many things that my family and my friends might find unkind or un-
fair?

Have I failed to add to my life the little niceties that make it so
much more interesting: learning a new skill, having a new hobby,
taking time for improving my health and the way I look, walk, talk
and generally appear to others? Am I learning that life need not be
as dull as I have allowed mine to become?

While I am proud of the way I deal with people outside our home,
do I always treat the members of my own family with respect and
courtesy? Aren't there many times in the course of the day when I
can give them little proofs of my approval and love? Am I really
ready to give up my longtime habit of blaming others for everything
that goes wrong or that I disapprove of?

Have I suddenly realized that I do too much talking? Do I let any-
one else be heard? Do I constantly interrupt and take control of a
conversation? I might find I could enjoy listening, perhaps learning a
new idea, a fresh point of view.

Faults like these, as I might describe them to myself, certainly in-
fluence the quality of life around me. They can be overcome, once I
have made myself entirely ready for this Step and the one that fol-
lows it.

A Step-Six Story

I had the good fortune to marry an alcoholic. Otherwise, I'd
have lived my whole life through without ever finding out what
something called "Al-Anon" could do to make me into a different
person—to remodel, repair and rehabilitate me. With my attitude
toward life and people, it's a wonder even a far-gone alcoholic
would choose me for a companion. Maybe it was I that chose him;

I was so strong-willed I was sure I could make something out of him. Our problem was not Jim's alcoholism, although that made things much worse. It was my own background, and what it had made of me, that caused the biggest part of our troubles.

I was brought up by an aunt whose God was money. Her philosophy of life was, "Money is the only friend you can trust; if you have money, you don't need friends." She taught me that the principal virtue of life was to work and save. Everything had to fit into that idea. She denied herself and her family whatever she thought was a luxury, and that included just about everything. So I grew up believing that buying anything but bare necessities meant wasting money. Going to movies, having nice clothes, etc., interfered with working and pinching pennies. It was a pretty thin existence, but I was so brain-washed that I felt a lot smarter than people who spent their money on frills, entertainment and other so-called nonsense.

I carried this rigid attitude into my adulthood and used it in fighting the battle with Jim's drinking. When nothing came of all my determination, I finally worked up enough courage to get myself to an Al-Anon meeting. I'd read about it in a column in our local paper, and although it was hard for me to believe the kind of magic talked about, I thought I owed it to myself to try it. It wasn't an easy step to take. All I could picture was a bunch of strangers who couldn't care less about me and my problems.

It didn't take long for that picture to change. In spite of my shying away from new people, I was drawn into the circle by their frank and loving sharing, the explanations, the willingness to help me. It took a while, but gradually I relaxed a little and did some sharing too. That was the beginning of my getting rid of the "old" me.

But there were still more good things in store for me. A patient sponsor, who really knew how to use the program, started me on the Twelve Steps. And did I stumble on those Steps! Of course I knew about God and that people prayed to Him and went to church and all that. But I had been trained to depend only on my self and the almighty dollar, so I thought people who were dependent were weaklings. And here I was being told that I'd have to recognize a Power that was to direct my life! With a kind of desperation I accepted this idea, but only half-heartedly, as I realized much later.

By the time I came to Step Six, I was finally convinced that there was no escape from the Higher Power, that God really does have a vital place in my life. I knew then and admitted that I would never become what I wanted to be without a close dependence on God. I learned much in Al-Anon. I learned about love, about the need to give and accept it freely. And at last I saw, much more clearly than when I was examining my shortcomings, how cold and shallow my whole attitude toward life had been.

It was a hard dicipline all along the way, but the new me that has emerged is a lot easier and more pleasant to live with than the one who blundered into Al-Anon, all weighted down with prejudice and material concerns. Money is no longer the most important thing to me.

STEP SEVEN

Humbly asked Him to remove our shortcomings.

Our work with Steps Four, Five and Six—the search, the admitting and the making-ready—put us in a position to relinquish self-will and experience the will of a Power greater than our own; all we needed to do was bring our freely-acknowledged faults to the God of our understanding and humbly *ask* to have them taken away.

"Humility is a greatly misunderstood quality. It is not weakness; it is strength. It does not mean submission, resignation or compliance; all these imply we still have lurking reservations. In humility, there is total willingness to accept God's help because we have finally been convinced that, without it, we cannot achieve our goals."[1] Humility is honesty and depth of vision, a realistic assessment of ourselves and our part in the scheme of things. It places us in a true relationship with a Higher Power. Before all else, we had stopped trying to control people and happenings in our daily experience. Our egos gave way to the Power in charge and the more we accepted that, the more we grew in the confident belief that there were other avenues open to us; we were no longer alone, we were no longer helpless, we could change, all we had to do was *ask*.

When all went well, we tried to be grateful; when things went badly, we reminded ourselves there would always be events over

[1]*AL-ANON FAMILY GROUPS*, Al-Anon Family Group Headquarters, Inc., Virginia Beach, VA. pg. 45.

which we had no control. How we reacted to these distresses was up to us and if we discovered new facets of our character that were not helpful to our recovery, we could turn again to our Higher Power. We did not need to fear our growing self-awareness because we could turn our thoughts to our spiritual source of help.

We could make this reaching out a continuous process, as continuous as our thoughts and feelings, acknowledging a sense of trust with each request. As our dependence on a Higher Power grew, we began to overcome the habit of relying only on ourselves. To rid ourselves of unwanted shortcomings, we learned to rely on assistance from a spiritual partner.

It wasn't important how we asked for help; each found a way to achieve this spiritual alliance. The importance lay in the act of asking. We had acted on our commitment and because we believed we could be helped, we were. Renewed by surrendering our shortcomings, we were ready to move forward to our recovery, to meet life each day without the weight of yesterday's defeats.

Thinking It Over

As I go through the Steps and earnestly try to use them, I find the experience, strength and hope of others who have taken the Steps before me. As I look into my own mirror, I see who I am—my strengths, my weaknesses; I don't have to be afraid to admit them to another human being. When I admit them to the God of my understanding, I am placing myself in the hands of a Power which can release me from a course of excessive self-sacrifice, or self-indulgence.

My path toward a new life was begun by my fearless inventory, and my commitment was reinforced by my willingness to face up to and admit my shortcomings.

Now, I am at a point where I can ask a spiritual partner to take away these shortcomings—I can give them away and give in to a new reality. Freedom from my old shortcomings offers me a new opportunity to learn better ways of thinking and doing. I can begin to concentrate on the qualities I would like to have in place of my shortcomings.

I don't expect to reach perfection. What might such perfection mean? Since such a goal is beyond me, I will settle for the simple, reasonable one of getting comfortable with myself. I will try to do, each day, each hour, what I can to strive forward toward self-improvement.

A Seventh-Step Story

In the years I have been in Al-Anon, the Steps have been increasingly important to my recovery. This past summer I had a terrible problem overcoming my anger toward a particular person.

Friends began to tell me I was obsessed with this person because I talked about my fury so much. I honestly realized they were right but I could not seem to shake the terrible feelings. One night, over ice cream, a very special friend suggested that I sit and write a list of all the things I resented. Then we would go over the list together and see what I could do about it. I sat down, admitted to my Higher Power, which I choose to call "God," the exact nature of my feelings. Then I listed them. It was painful; many of my feelings were distorted or contradictory, some were valid.

I began to dissect my attitudes and in looking at the list, many of the indignities were revealed as absurd or petty; these I was able to dismiss. I did not want to cling to the same way of thinking and acting. I wanted to be able to handle situations concerning this person with poise and serenity.

My friend was dear and special and sat through all this patiently and lovingly. I cried, I yelled, I justified and I was drained. Yes, I was ready for the Seventh Step. I was able to humbly ask to have this particular shortcoming removed. I had searched and I had become ready. Finally, I asked God, "Please, remove my anger!"

I was totally prepared to receive help and the pain was gone. A Power greater than myself had removed it. I had been able to humbly surrender my will. I had been helped. The Seventh Step had been the means to healing a very painful cancer in my soul.

STEP EIGHT

Made a list of all persons we had harmed, and became willing to make amends to them all.

It was sometimes difficult for us to determine how something we had done could have hurt someone else—or what hidden motives we might have had for what we had done—or even why we should make amends.

We needed to do something specific, take pencil in hand and write down the names of certain people.

Accepting this discipline with complete honesty, may have caused us some pain, but we found the result well worth it, for it promised us nothing less than a clear conscience and better understanding of ourselves. Taking this Step helped us get rid of guilt. Although the guilt may have been deeply hidden in our subconscious, Step Eight gave us courage to bring it into the daylight and, later, to do whatever would free us from the pain inflicted on us by our past actions. By doing our courageous best with this Step, we began to feel more comfortable with ourselves.

There were questions to ask ourselves: What did we do that hurt someone? Why did we do it? What were the consequences? Did it do permanent damage? Were there single instances in which we were unfair, unkind, deceitful, selfish, or hurtful? Or, could it be that we were putting too much weight on something the other person wasn't even disturbed by?

One answer sufficed. If something we did in the past had left us with a feeling of gnawing guilt, then the name of the person we had hurt was added to our list helping us to keep in mind the purpose of Step Eight, which was to relieve us of painful and embarrassing memories which generated this guilt. This could be done only by being willing to make amends in some way.

We may have been tempted to justify what we did by thinking, "But I did that only because of what she did to me," or "I really only meant to help him get sober; how could I know it was going to turn out that way?" We could not let ourselves take refuge in excuses, or Step Eight would not have done its best work for us.

We might have imagined that a wrong we did was due to some character flaw in us, but this wasn't always so. Much damage can be done by those richly endowed with kindness, love, sympathy and tolerance. Many a person with all those beautiful qualities and with the best of intentions has wreaked havoc on the lives of others and themselves.

One area in which most of us found ample opportunity to put this Step into practice was in our family relationships. Here again, love and concern for husband or wife, children, or parents, did not always assure our being good to them. Over-protection might have deprived them of opportunities for growth. The trials and stresses of living with an alcoholic certainly may have distorted our perspectives.

Loud, bitter quarrels may have done untold damage, undermining feelings of security and generating hatred for others. Where such a situation existed, we may have had a good deal of amending to do. It is often the non-drinking parent the children resent most bitterly. If they have heard angry reproaches, if we have made them suffer for our frustrations, they may have felt an even warmer relationship to the alcoholic than to the other parent, whose behavior seemed to them even more irrational. Moreover, if we have set a poor example for our children, we need not be surprised if sometimes they behaved badly.

Such things, too, had to be taken into consideration when we made a list of those to whom we owed amends.

If we were inclined to think back to the wrong we did to the alcoholic and others before we embraced the Al-Anon program, we could take comfort from all we were learning about acceptance, detachment, understanding—and how to love without demanding conformity from others. This armory of personal improvements gave us the strength we needed to make amends, not only to the living, but to the departed, by being kind to others and forgiving of ourselves. The wisdom and confidence we gained from our study of Al-Anon principles helped us avoid repeating our past mistakes. That, in itself, was a kind of amending for past wrongs.

There was, yet, one more way: To teach ourselves to be aware of others' needs, by being compassionate when they hurt, allowing them to build self-esteem and sharing our strength with them.

Finally, what about the harm we had inflicted on ourselves through the years, our suffering because of errors of judgement, our willfulness and other shortcomings? Most of us had many amends to make to ourselves now that we had found the way to improve our lives.

Thinking It Over

Step Eight is a "clean-slate" Step. Taking it can dispose of many discomforts. It isn't that there is total healing in making the effort to recall those I have harmed; perhaps, even making amends can't do that, but it can be a relief to acknowledge where I went wrong and hurt people. (Sometimes it was due to my being distracted and disturbed by the alcoholic problem; perhaps due to my being envious or resentful, and maybe just in disagreement with somebody.)

Those causes of unkindness, which I recognize as flaws in my character, came to my attention when I was working with Step Four. Whenever I start thinking about the people I have hurt, I keep backtracking to Step Four. Perhaps I have overlooked some of my major shortcomings, the "hurting weapons" that have led me into being unkind to people.

I realized, when I remembered some of the things I had done, that I hadn't put enough emphasis on those character flaws. Now in Step Eight, I can face them and be willing to make amends for everything those flaws have led me into.

I can stop being an enthusiastic critic of other people's shortcomings, their actions, ideas, ways of talking, appearance. I no longer need to feed that desire to feel superior. I can remind myself how hurtful such behavior can be by imagining how miserable I would feel if anyone said or did such things to me. I can make amends to those who were the objects of my gossiping, by not repeating things that are often nothing but untrue rumors. I see all this more clearly each time I work with Step Eight. I can list the names of those for whom I have shown a lack of concern and a total inability to feel how they were hurt by what I was saying and doing. I can ask my Higher Power to take a hand and help me to look at what I have done to others. If I want to be loved, I must learn to love. Strange, how the faults I was least able to acknowledge caused me so much trouble. Mine had hurt many people. I will try to put them all on my list and pray to be guided to the best ways of making amends to them all.

A Step-Eight Story

I had kind of an unusual experience with Step Eight. The fact is, I didn't do a very good job on that Step and I didn't realize it until after I'd painstakingly completed the whole Twelve. I had to take some pretty embarrassing punishment for neglecting what I should have done with Step Eight.

I'd failed to do some really hard thinking about the people I'd hurt in my pre-Al-Anon days. Actually I didn't even make much of a list. I just thought of some of the people I had treated badly and needed to make amends to, and I did it—after a fashion. It seemed all right at the time, but as I continued my work with the Steps, I could see where I had slipped.

Before I came into Al-Anon, when my reaction to my husband's drinking was driving me into insanity, we had been long-time friends with another couple, Tom and Terry. Tom was an alcoholic, too. Well, the way I behaved made it more comfortable for my husband to spend his time elsewhere, and he spent a lot of it at Tom's house. When we were having our fights, I used to challenge him about always visiting someone else instead of his own family. His answer was usually something like, "Well, if you weren't always raising so much hell, I might feel more like staying home once in a while."

That gave me an excuse to blame his drinking on somebody else, and I'd say, "Maybe you wouldn't drink so much if you didn't spend so much time with that drunk, Tom. I don't know how Terry puts up with it."

I had the thought—it had been brewing in my mind for a long time—that maybe part of the attraction of Tom's place might be Terry herself, so I added jealousy to my other insanities. When the four of us went out together, which we still did occasionally, I'd watch the two of them like a hawk to see how they were behaving toward one another. I finally decided that they were having an affair. So I also took on the dramatic role of the betrayed wife.

Things got rapidly worse, and one day, practically beside myself with rage, I called her up and accused her of what I suspected. She was indignant, really furious, which was unusual for her quiet personality. "I won't even bother to deny that," she said. "I have an alcoholic of my own and I certainly don't need another. Maybe if you'd find a way to control your temper, your husband wouldn't be so anxious to leave the house every time he gets a chance. You know, it isn't always convenient for us to have him around so much, but I feel sorry for the poor guy." And with that, she said a quiet goodbye and hung up.

My bitterness and resentment lasted a long time, even after I knew that there hadn't been the least bit of truth in my accusation of Terry. Life got worse and worse . . . and then, one wonderful day, the door of Al-Anon opened to me.

That was about six years ago and I needn't tell you how everything has changed. Looking back, I'd done a lot of damage to a number of people, and I tried hard to make up for it. But why that broken friendship with Terry never came to mind, I don't know. I really must have had it buried deep, and since they had moved away to another suburb, there wasn't anything current to call it to mind.

One day, going through our local supermarket, we came face-to-face with each other. I was covered with confusion and embarrassment, I didn't know what to say, and the whole memory of that awful time came flooding back. And along with it, the word AMEND shouting at me mentally. I just walked over to her and held out my hand. And she took it.

As we began to renew our friendship, I learned that her husband Tom had recently found himself in AA, but strangely, she had not thought seriously about Al-Anon, although she had heard about it. That gave me my opportunity to make some real, practical amends, by explaining what Al-Anon had done for me. Out of curiosity, she started attending meetings. Now we have a solid friendship that I know will last and grow.

STEP NINE

Made direct amends to such people wherever possible, except when to do so would injure them or others.

Somebody once compared taking Step Nine to taking a dose of bitter medicine and then feeling wonderful afterward. It's an exacting Step, but taking it gave us practical, realistic ways to decide how amends are to be made.

A key word in this Step is "direct." This helped us avoid evading the issue when we were tempted to choose the kind of amends that would be least painful or embarrassing to us. "Wherever possible," the amends were made directly to the person we had harmed. It was up to us to decide, with scrupulous honesty, whether making amends was possible or not.

Once we had made a list of those we had injured, it was up to us to choose an appropriate way to make up for what we did. If it was something like thoughtless gossip or unkind criticism, perhaps a sincere apology might have helped.

Frankly admitting we were wrong in what we said or did may have mended the breach without making a big thing of it. But even minor situations should be carefully thought over before taking any step toward redressing a wrong. It may be wise to ask ourselves some questions.

Would an apology open an old wound? Is this the right moment to make good the hurt that was inflicted? Might we be tempted to brush off our conduct because the person offended was someone

we didn't care much about anyway? With the help of others, we
found that our likes and dislikes had nothing to do with our obligation to make amends. One of the purposes of Step Nine is to
gain peace of mind for ourselves by erasing our feelings of guilt.
This is, in one sense, making amends to ourselves, not to be
overlooked when we are working with Step Nine.

The problem becomes more difficult when something we did or
said resulted in serious, perhaps irreversible problems for others.
These unkindnesses are harder to acknowledge, even after we
bring them to the surface of our minds; however, it is necessary to
our own peace of mind to review exactly what we did that caused
the damage.

Perhaps we were too free with advice which, in the end, actually
increased difficulties for the one we were trying to help. We might
have been tempted to excuse ourselves by thinking, "I meant well,
and anyway, he didn't have to take my advice." Such evasion still
left us with the full weight of responsibility for making whatever
amends were possible.

Having created painful consequences or injuries were actions we
wanted to face up to before we could find real peace of mind.
Where the children of a family were affected, they, too, needed to
be considered when making amends. All such matters were carefully examined and handled, because in trying to make amends,
we didn't want to make things worse.

In every word and action that violated the Golden Rule, to do
unto others as we would have them do unto us, there were amends
to make.

Many of us in Al-Anon realized that among the important amends
are those we owed to that very alcoholic we blamed for all the
problems that beset us in the past. Before we began to live by

the Al-Anon program, it was difficult for us to admit we might have been at fault. Yet, we realized that what we did, before we knew better, may still have to be faced.

Whatever the outcome of those years of living with alcoholism, whether sobriety, separation or reunion, it was important for us to confront what we had done through bitterness and frustration. Here again, honesty and good judgment provided the key.

Many relationships to which alcoholism once brought dissension and misery may still be mended. We found many an occasion in our daily lives when we could convey our regrets to the alcoholic, other family members and our friends, tactfully, maybe with a bit of humor, to avoid reviving painful memories of the drinking days. We also made amends when we showed interest in another's well-being, activities and achievements. Thoughtful courtesies suggested a basic change in our own attitudes and the way we behaved toward others. More gentleness, tolerance and acceptance along with our own sense of dignity did much to restore inner harmony.

In some cases, it seemed best to do nothing. Whatever we might have wished to do to relieve ourselves of guilt over the past could have resulted in more hurt for those to whom we wished to make amends. In other cases, we might never have found ways to make amends.

What if the husband, wife, father, mother, child or friend was no longer there to receive the amends we were longing to make? There was a comforting alternative: In learning to think of others, to consider their feelings and well-being, taking conscious care to be thoughtful and generous, we could equate our growth in the program to the amends we could not make to those who were gone. This process of loving remembrance served as a reminder of what we wanted to be, how we wanted to relate to everyone in our lives. Little by little, this remembering helped us to do better each day.

Further, this Step showed us a concrete way to make amends for harm we may have done to ourselves. We learned to forgive ourselves when we realized that growth is a gradual process.

No matter what our relationships were or what actions we were contemplating in our attempts to fulfill Step Nine, a sincere effort to make good helped us find the most just and satisfying way do to it.

Thinking It Over

Step Nine, it seems to me, has a specific message for me. It says: In this Step I am very much on my own; it is up to me to decide how its key words and phrases apply to my life.

First, I must be truly willing, as Step Eight suggests, even when I foresee that my amends might be rejected. The important thing is to make them, whether I am forgiven or not.

What form are my direct amends going to take in each case? Might I be tempted to sidestep when it would be embarrassing or humiliating to admit to the wrong I did? How can I be sure I wouldn't be lifting the lid of Pandora's box of troubles for somebody?

One thing is certain, this Step is a test of my honesty. And like the other Steps, it reminds me of the importance of humility. Finally, if I can do Step Nine full justice, I will have brought myself to the threshold of the three spiritual Steps which follow it.

Perhaps no one is entirely free of regret for past mistakes; I know I am not and I can foresee a welcome release from my uneasiness when I acknowledge the hurts I have inflicted on others.

When I take action on this Step with friends or even relatives, the amends may not be too painful to make. One way might simply be to change my attitude toward them, to be more uncritical and loving. Sometimes this may be better than to stir up memories of past injuries which, if not too serious, may have been forgotten. A wholesome change in my way of behaving toward them may be all that is needed to make us comfortable with each other.

I thought it would be a good idea to review what I learned about myself when I was working on Step Four, because I suddenly realized that many of the wrongs I did to others grew out of the shortcomings I had discovered earlier. If I was intolerant, it may have been caused by a habit of being resentful. I might have been hurtful because of envy. Selfishness or greed may have led me to taking unfair advantage of someone.

Realizing this, and my efforts to overcome my own faults, helps me to understand how I came to hurt others. Making amends is still another step toward healing myself.

A Step-Nine Story

A visiting speaker told this story about an Al-Anon friend he had sponsored and how his friend had faced a problem for which Step Nine gave him the answer.

The friend had a younger sister to whom he was devoted. When she grew up, she married a man who turned out to be an alcoholic, and soon she became one herself. He and his family knew nothing about alcoholism as a disease. They tried everything they could think of to get her to stop drinking. Of course, they were all the wrong things, including trying to force her to leave her husband, thinking that would automatically cure her. Finally both he and his parents gave up and angrily cut off all communication with her.

Although he went along with it, he always felt uneasy and guilty, but he was torn between loyalty to his parents and to his sister. He excused himself by thinking it was a hopeless case, but that didn't help much.

Later, in his own marriage, he suddenly discovered that one of his own teenagers had a drinking problem. After a good deal of agonizing, somebody persuaded him to try Al-Anon. What an awakening that was! All the painful memories of his estranged sister came flooding back and with it a great remorse over his long neglect of her. It was when he started Step Nine that he decided he'd have to do something to make amends. First, he had to search for her to find out where and how she was living. Although he dreaded what he might discover, he was still determined to reach out to her. To his relief, when he found her, she was sober in AA, self-supporting and with her two sons in Alateen. Both her boys were already helping out with part-time jobs.

She welcomed him with open arms; the bitterness she had felt about the family had been overcome by her living the AA program.

What could he do, he wondered, to make amends to her for his past rejection. As sister and brother renewed their childhood affection and understanding, their friendship grew. When he learned that there would be no possibility of her being able to send her boys to college, it gave him the idea to make direct amends that could change the lives of all of them for the better. He promised his sister that he would undertake the education of both boys; their joy was as great as his own. In his decision to help others, he found the greatest benefit was to himself.

STEP TEN

Continued to take personal inventory and when we were wrong promptly admitted it.

The earlier Steps, and especially, Steps Four through Nine prepared us for Step Ten. Through those Steps, we acknowledged the importance of recognizing our shortcomings and admitting them. Then, we learned that our self-observing and self-evaluating was to continue, confirming the basic purpose of the Twelve Steps as a way of life.

Our striving for fulfillment went on and on, as we taught ourselves to recognize the meaning and purpose of everything we did. It was less difficult if we made an honest effort to absorb and use the earlier Steps. The underlying thought was that we had already come a long way in the process of improving our lives. A continuing review became easier because we had been geared up for it by our earlier efforts. We had an ever-clearer picture of what we were really like and what we wanted to change. This self-knowledge came all the more readily when it was bolstered by our willingness to correct our mistakes as soon as they happened. Old habits of thought and action became less automatic and compelling, and each one we overcame paid rich dividends in self-knowledge. When we came to recognize we had done something unwise, unkind, or ungenerous, we didn't feel quite easy until we had corrected the error.

There was a valuable bonus in devoting ourselves to Step Ten: It helped us realize that the errors we made hurt us. Surely none of us wanted our spiritual progress hampered by having unamended errors weighing on our conscience. We were not comfortable when we found ourselves in a situation we had created—and wished we hadn't. When we were aware we had reacted through selfishness, resentment, or any other fault, it reminded us that these short-comings were not entirely rooted out in our work with Steps Four through Seven. Lapses hurt us, perhaps, even more than they hurt others, but they could also be lessons for growth. That was the best reason for keeping ourselves alert to what we were doing and say-ing, and promptly correcting whatever lapses our faults had led us into.

A thoughtful consideration convinced us that our views of a person or a situation were not necessarily infallible. If we could not accept the right of others to see things differently, we might have blundered into problems, and those would be problems of our own making. Taking Step Ten gave us the opportunity to spare ourselves the consequences of being stubbornly opinionated. It reminded us that we were not all-wise, that the philosophy of our Steps is based on humility, on acknowledging a Power greater than ourselves.

Step Ten asks us to continue to take action to wipe the slate clean, to avoid building up regrets, showing us again that the Al-Anon program is centered on us, on developing our own content-ment with life. This leads us to still another thought: not to allow ourselves to be affected, or influenced, by the demands and expec-tations of others. In our relationships with family and friends, we may have felt we were only trying to please when we did what someone else thought we should. We thought we were being un-selfish when we put aside our own preferences and went along meekly with what somebody else wanted of us. What we were really doing was damaging ourselves, and for this, too, we needed the constant reminder of Step Ten. Perhaps, we were afraid to refuse a request or demand; afraid to cross someone, especially if it was the alcoholic who was trying to manipulate and control; in standing our ground we were not only helping others realize that they could not impose their unreasonable behavior on us, but we were properly protecting our own right to what was best for us. Being aware of that right served a dual, beneficial purpose and strengthened us to meet our predicaments with courage and confidence.

The basic message of Step Ten added up to just this: We need to keep observing what we did and why we did it. Examining our motives provides us with the tools we need to free ourselves of many problems that had beset us in the past.

Thinking It Over

I think of Step Ten as being a detailed method of fulfilling the ancient saying, "Know thyself." The self I want to know would never be uncaring, selfish or condemning of others. If I feel there is something I ought to be sorry for, particularly if it resulted in hurting someone, I will not try to avoid facing my responsibility by thinking, "I was right in what I did," or "They deserved it." I will keep in mind that I was not assigned to judge others, that my views, even those deeply ingrained in me, should not be applied to them.

Whenever I decide I am in the wrong, I will be doing myself a good turn when I promptly admit it.

When I was thinking through the meaning of this Step and how I could best put it into action, I thought of some questions to ask myself as a kind of review:

Do I set aside a little time each day for thinking about myself, my feelings about the people I live with and meet, and my behavior toward them? Have I tried to use the power of gentleness and courtesy toward others, especially those close to me? Do I keep in mind that the authority I have over my children should be used with love and tenderness? Do I realize that this can make them more responsive to my guidance? Can I be comfortable with myself when I have let my temper explode, when I lash out at people without considering the consequences? Have I wondered what I'd look like in a mirror while this was going on? How do I feel when I learn that someone has made an unkind comment about me? How do I react? Ignore it? Lash out? Or try to forgive knowing that I myself still have faults to overcome?

What can I do to rid myself of personal prejudices about people of a different race, nationality or religious faith? Or against those who don't hold the same views as mine about social and political matters? Wouldn't I like myself better if I could really live and let live?

A Tenth-Step Story

The period just before I fall asleep seems the best time for me to take the Tenth Step. I find it easier to do it on a regular basis at the same time each day.

In taking a fearless and searching Fourth-Step inventory I didn't have to search too deeply to see the lengths to which I had gone to please people. I had reached the point where, if I talked to people and saw disapproval registered in their face, I would change what I was saying midstream and tell them what I thought they wanted to hear. As I worked on changing myself through the application of the Sixth and Seventh Steps, I started risking disfavor by being more honest. I began to tell people how I felt. It wasn't easy to allow others to see the anger or insecurity I had concealed for so long. I thought the whole world would see the real me with the volcano buried inside. They'll see that she isn't the nice, sweet person who always had a smile and a kind word. The first time someone pushed in front of me on a line and I said, "Excuse me, I think I'm next," the words rang hollow in my ears as my face reddened. When I told my husband I was keeping the dress he disliked, my heart dropped and my knees went weak as he stalked out of the room.

Several years passed. Expressing my real feelings almost became a habit, a regular part of my life. Standing up for my rights continually became easier with practice. Very often at night, when I reviewed the day's happenings, I would congratulate myself for the tremendous strides I had made towards working on my defects and shortcomings of approval-seeking and people-pleasing. I marveled at my ability to say, "No." My husband, who balked at first, also commented positively on the change in my behavior. Spurred on by the good feelings, I continued to assert myself more and more. There were times I didn't even recognize myself as the timid woman who entered Al-Anon many years before.

Then, after awhile, a feeling of discomfort returned. As I reviewed the day's happenings I didn't feel as pleased with myself. Vague images and recollections flashed before me of daily scenes with shopkeepers, phone callers, friends and members of my family. Was I being positive with that shoe salesman this afternoon or was I just being rude? Did I need to be so abrupt with that person on the telephone? Was I keeping that blouse that my husband didn't care for just to prove that he wasn't going to have his way? He was not going to control me anymore, I bristled. Suddenly it seemed that I had begun asserting myself to the point of defiance, even to the point of aggression.

One bone of contention between my husband and me concerned family gatherings. At first if he didn't want to go with me, I stayed home. Then, I started to go alone. This worked for awhile; it was even an improvement. But the pendulum swung so far in the other direction that not only was I often unreasonable, many times I was cutting off my nose to spite my face. Holidays, when I desperately craved our togetherness, I was off and running by myself.

These realizations that came during my nightly spot-check, the Tenth-Step inventory, didn't hit all at once. It was many nights of uneasy feelings, many nights thinking, "Something's not right, there's something I have to change," that brought the picture of the new me into focus.

Fortunately, I was able to put balance back into my life before what I thought was my new "assertiveness" became more of a character defect than the one I originally was trying to overcome. When I saw how I was acting, I was able to soften and change my behavior with people around me. I could also talk to my husband and explain what was happening.

I was also grateful that taking the Tenth Step helped me promptly admit I was wrong. This didn't come easily. Many nights I would find excuses for my behavior, but the constant application of this Step taught me how to say, "I made a mistake."

STEP ELEVEN

Sought through prayer and meditation to improve our conscious contact with God as we understood Him, praying only for knowledge of His will for us and the power to carry that out.

If we had reason to be impressed with the helping Power in taking the earlier Steps, taking the Eleventh, for many of us, opened the door to "a new heaven and a new earth."

Study of its inner meaning brought many of us closer to a Power greater than ourselves. Each part of this Step had a way of enlightening us, giving us insight, showing us people, problems and life in a new perspective. It was up to us to learn how we could best fit the Step to our needs. Each word and phrase reflects a particular sharing.

We were searching for a life more rich in purpose and satisfaction. This meant seeking to understand more clearly the part our own attitude played in determining what happened to us in our everyday life.

How did we do this seeking? Through prayer and meditation. These were the means by which we learned to use our spiritual resources in solving our difficulties and making decisions, large and small. When we tried to find solutions in a purely analytical way, by what we thought of as "figuring things out," the results were apt to be disappointing. We needed the help of a wisdom greater than our own.

The purpose of prayer and meditation was to improve our con-

scious contact with God—the God of our own understanding.
Here the key word was "conscious," making ourselves deeply, viv-
idly aware of the Higher Power that has such a vital place in our
lives.

The word "prayer," as a direct communication with that Power,
appears for the first time in Step Eleven. For some of us, prayer
was our promise to surrender to God's will. When we were truly
willing, it gave us confidence that our needs would be met in the
way that was best for us. For, as Step Eleven confirms, prayer
was not asking for what we wanted or felt we deserved, but only
for "knowledge of His Will for us."

The word, "meditation," simply means concentrated thought on
a chosen subject, thinking or considering quietly, soberly and
deeply, and focusing one's thoughts on something in order to
understand it deeply. For many, it is serious and sustained reflection, or mental contemplation of a spiritual truth. Thus, when we
meditated, we shut out all distractions and disturbing thoughts
about problems and irritations and brought our minds to bear on a
single idea. It might have been a phrase, a thought from something
we had heard or read; or, it might have been a specific object we
could picture in our minds.

It was not easy to fix our attention on one idea in this way; at
first, it took real effort to keep our thoughts from wandering to
other topics or, more often, to revert to our daily trivia or decision-
making. It was helpful, perhaps even necessary for some of us, to
allot a specific time for our daily meditation. It was then that new
insights were unfolded to us.

Some were amazed to find an idea flashing into our minds that
we'd never before thought of, along with the conviction that it was
the right answer. Having been provided with such unexpected

guidance, we could believe, too, that we would be given "the power to carry that out."

Thinking It Over

I can begin to use the Eleventh Step with a good deal of assurance. With what I have learned in Al-Anon, I can try, for example, to concentrate on thinking about God and letting Him tell me what to do.

I want to be able to let God into my life. There may be a lot of stubborn resistance to overcome before I can relate to, or understand a divine, universal, all-powerful idea.

I can make myself sit quietly and make myself ready to communicate with confidence with the God of my understanding.

"Going it alone" for many years has brought me much trouble and frustration. One kind of deep trouble finally brought me to Al-Anon. Even then, I started out by embracing the idea that my God was my Al-Anon group, my friends, who were doing so much to help me.

Little by little, I am able to accept the thought that my life has always been dependent on a Higher Power and as I gradually give up my willful denial, I may be able to feel a spiritual influence working in every part of my life. I am brought to this realization by one word in the Eleventh Step, "improve." My conscious contact with God is far from complete; indeed, it may never be. It has to be improved continually, and the only way I can improve it, is by sharpening my awareness of His presence. Prayer and meditation is not just an occasional activity to be done when I need it, or happen to think of it, but a consistent, unswerving use of my thinking faculties to make myself more and more conscious of God's part in everything I think, say, and do.

As my effort becomes a daily exercise, I can actually feel my growing nearness to that Power so much greater than I.

An Eleventh-Step Story

I believe that Step Eleven can be used constantly—every minute. Once you've established a certain way of thinking, it becomes a habit that gives new meaning to everything in life. There is not one moment when you are not using, or experiencing, in some way, one of God's miracles, only "miracle" isn't the word, because what I am thinking of is not the exceptional, unusual, or rare phenomena, but the ordinary experiences we have all the time. What makes miracles of these commonplaces is our seeing what's before us as God-created.

It means no longer taking for granted the familiar things of life that we never used to give a passing thought to, something as routine as a breakfast of orange juice, eggs, buttered toast and coffee. They have converged upon our table from the far corners of the country or the world, each achieving its intricate character by means of something no mere human could devise. The bright oranges on their trees, drinking in sunshine and health for us; the ingenuity of man that transported them into our reach. And surely it isn't hard to think of an egg in terms of a miracle, that combination of nutritional elements, vitamins and proteins all neatly protected in its shell. Or the wheat that made the bread, drawing its special sustenance out of the earth for us, the complexity of the cow that gave us the butter. All this could only have been created by a Power far greater than we are.

When we habitually think in this way, we develop a constant awareness, a constant wonder, at how we are being cared for by that Power. The things we use and wear, the materials needed for our jobs—we tend to regard them as man-made, but when you think back to the source, what did man use to make them? And where did it all come from, so perfectly adapted to its purpose?

Let's think, too, about the way circumstances often come together in totally unplanned, unexpected ways to help us out of a dilemma, or to help us learn a new point of view. Consider, too, the selfless kindness of our friends, especially in a fellowship like ours—all of this, it seems to me, is a part of a plan I cannot understand, but accept with deep gratitude and humility.

STEP TWELVE

Having had a spiritual awakening as the result of these Steps, we tried to carry this message to others, and to practice these principles in all our affairs.

Here in Step Twelve comes the culmination of the spiritual nature of our shared experience. Whether we have realized it or not, we have had a rebirth of the spirit throughout our participation in Al-Anon.

It is the kind of spiritual rebirth that many of us have shared, and will continue to share in the future as we absorb the inner meaning of the Twelve Steps and learn to live by them. We feel this can come about for others as it did for us when we devoted ourselves with all our hearts to the daily practice of these principles.

Have we had a spiritual awakening? Were we able to "practice these principles in all our affairs?" Were we ready and willing to "carry this message to others?" The words of this Step sum up everything we feel we needed in our search for a good life. We still feel that way.

Surely we have come a long way from that first despairing time when we finally realized we had to let go of the problems that were overwhelming us. We were compelled to "admit we were powerless."

The Steps between were our re-education, changing the attitudes and reactions that grew out of our painful confusion. Taking them gave us the confidence that comes from relying on a Power greater than ourselves.

What could a spiritual awakening really do for us? It could set us free. Not free of problems; those we will always have as part of our human condition. Our release came from knowing that help was always within our reach. We needed only to ask and accept. This was the dependable way to get help, whether our difficulties came from living with alcoholism or any other situation in which we have reacted in self-defeating ways.

Having studied and used the Steps, we can now say with confidence we have become better people, with a clearer view of our problems and what we can do about them. This is a gift, a pattern for living that really works. It it our reward for the courage and determination we applied in using the Steps to change ourselves.

We shall continue to try to carry this message to others. This was and is our opportunity to repay the good we received. Carrying the message to others has spread Al-Anon's help to troubled people all over the world. When we fulfill that responsibility, our reward is an ever richer gift.

We learned, too, the importance of gratitude. To acknowledge what someone has done for us is a wholesome response that makes all of us feel good. We wanted to return the kindness in some way, but real gratitude required more than that of us. It made us want to offer kind and friendly service to others as well. Each day we find ample opportunity for this in our fellowship, where so many lonely, confused and troubled people need to be comforted by our loving concern and our willingness to share the help we have received. We find it is not enough merely to attend meetings regularly, or even to accept an office in the group. Carrying the message means personal one-to-one sharing with one another. It means giving moral support, standing by and listening, without criticizing or condemning, to the troubles and misfortunes of another person, and helping him or her to find the path we have found. It means sharing love and experience with the unhappy newcomer who blames another for everything that went wrong, just as we used to do before our eyes were opened. It means being willing to help the long-time member who still finds it hard to apply the principles of the program to daily living.

It does not mean solving problems for others, but helping them to solve their own, without giving advice that might seem right to us but might not be right for them. Some of us may have found it difficult to think about others in this way, especially when we were beset with problems of our own, but failure in this would have deprived us of valuable experience. Not only does giving help make us feel good about ourselves, but sharing the burden of others often generates gratitude and love in them so they want to help others in turn.

Did we perhaps think we were too busy with our daily concerns to think about the needs of someone else? If we were self-conscious or timid, we found it difficult to open the door to communication. If we tried to be receptive, people with problems were only too eager to ask for help. No matter what kept us from reaching out a helping hand, we could at least try, and when we did try to reach the hearts of others, inviting their confidence in us, we discovered that we had done as much for ourselves as for someone else. An ancient Buddhist philosopher put it this way: "There is no such thing as sacrifice. There is opportunity to serve and he who overlooks it, robs only himself."

We found our Twelfth Step continued with another thought: that our effort could be carried still further, toward practicing these principles in all our affairs. The principles are, of course, those guides which we discovered by taking the Steps. We were brought back once again to judge whatever we did or said or even thought, by the standards we had accepted through our work with the Twelve Steps. Many of us had to remind ourselves of the hazard of discouragement. We had a tendency to slip back into old habits and familiar faults. But we had only to look back to our beginnings in Al-Anon to reassure ourselves. We never gave up, and we continue to renew, one day at a time, our striving to improve our lives by repeated practice of the Steps and all they imply. This is truly living with the program. It means following Al-Anon principles each day and each hour, to guard ourselves against confusion. The more closely our thoughts relate to a Power greater than ourselves, the more we find we are growing in humility, without which there could be no spiritual progress.

Thinking It Over

I can think of Step Twelve as a compact summary of our entire program. Its first statement intimates what I am working toward: a spiritual awakening. To me that means to be able to see everything in life—people, things and happenings—in a spiritual light, in their relation to a Higher Power which I now choose to call God. Once I can reach that level, many things will become clear to me that never were before. I'll know instinctively what is right for me.

I can learn to share in meetings through learning about and experiencing God's love for me. In my gratitude, I can try to return that love to other people. I was selfish before Al-Anon. When I go to meetings I can give, by my very presence, encouragement to the new person. In making calls and in sponsoring newcomers, I give patience and time. In every act of my Twelfth Step work, I'm giving . . . which simply means loving. This is what I have learned in Al-Anon, and the Al-Anons love me just as I am. This gives me hope. In carrying the message to others, I pray I'll always remember I can do even more for myself than I can do for them. Carrying the message is an obligation I have. Let me remind myself that what I do speaks louder than what I say.

Daily, I work the Twelve wonderful Steps and put into practice these principles in all my affairs.

A Twelfth-Step Story

When I reached the Twelfth Step, once again I stumbled. Initially it seemed so simple; a sort of summing up of the other eleven. I sighed with relief and ran to my sponsor with the good news that I had done it. I was through. "Read it again," she said, as she had so often before. Gradually over the months the three distinct parts of the Step came into focus.

Certainly, I had hoped for a dramatic sprirtual awakening, as some of us have had. But the Step says this awakening would come as a result of practicing the first eleven. There was to be no easy shortcut, just hard work with all the help I needed, right at hand. Many times the going was slow; sometimes it was tedious; occasionally it was painful. There was the time, for instance, a few years ago, after I had been a member of Al-Anon for awhile, that I literally turned my back on the spiritual power of this program. I still attended meetings but was only "talking a good game." The hurt I caused my family and myself was and is very real. But this very Power that I had failed did not fail me and gave me the tools to start again.

Now it is clear that, rather than experiencing one glorious moment, my growth will be gradual and it need never end.

So many people, in so many different ways, have tried to carry this message. Their sharing in meetings or on a one-to-one basis, their service at the group, District, Assembly or worldwide level ensured that Al-Anon was there the day I went to my first meeting, and will be there for the newcomer tomorrow. This generosity that enhances personal recovery, truly translates the phrase "I am responsible" from mere words into action, and it is what makes the Steps come alive. The truth of giving the program away in order to keep it was forcefully brought home to me when I offered to sponsor an Alateen group. I intended to give those young people what I had learned. Instead, for five years they refreshingly helped me to laugh at myself and taught me a great deal about maturity. They trusted me and proved it by their honesty. They showed me another facet of detachment, a lesson that proved invaluable in raising my own children. Finally, I learned from them a great deal about what real love is. What priceless gifts. (And *I* was going to give to them!)

Taking the last part of this Step meant I could try to practice these principles in all my affairs. Having serenity is a snap sitting around a table at a meeting. It is much more toilsome for me to attain it with my family or friends, in my job, with little things and, of course, with those people I knew who "didn't understand."

Having taken the Twelfth Step means I live these principles when I admit to my neighbor or boss I'm wrong, instead of rationalizing my behavior. I practice this program when I forgive a hurt rather than hold a grudge. When I make the time to listen to my child or to meditate, I'm really being good to myself. If I apply the Serenity Prayer to a trying situation, I'm the beneficiary.

I am nowhere near perfection and surely not yet done, as I naively thought I was, but each day that I try to work this Step is good and getting better.

Part II

THE TWELVE TRADITIONS

THE TWELVE TRADITIONS

Our group experience suggests that the unity of the Al-Anon Family Groups depends upon our adherence to these Traditions:

1. Our common welfare should come first; personal progress for the greatest number depends upon unity.
2. For our group purpose there is but one authority—a loving God as He may express Himself in our group conscience. Our leaders are but trusted servants; they do not govern.
3. The relatives of alcoholics, when gathered together for mutual aid, may call themselves an Al-Anon Family Group, provided that, as a group, they have no other affiliation. The only requirement for membership is that there be a problem of alcoholism in a relative or friend.
4. Each group should be autonomous, except in matters affecting another group or Al-Anon or AA as a whole.
5. Each Al-Anon Family Group has but one purpose: to help families of alcoholics. We do this by practicing the Twelve Steps of AA *ourselves,* by encouraging and understanding our alcoholic relatives, and by welcoming and giving comfort to families of alcoholics.
6. Our Al-Anon Family Groups ought never endorse, finance or lend our name to any outside enterprise, lest problems of money, property and prestige divert us from our primary spiritual aim. Although a separate entity, we should always cooperate with Alcoholics Anonymous.
7. Every group ought to be fully self-supporting, declining outside contributions.

8. Al-Anon Twelfth-Step work should remain forever nonprofessional, but our service centers may employ special workers.

9. Our groups, as such, ought never be organized; but we may create service boards or committees directly responsible to those they serve.

10. The Al-Anon Family Groups have no opinion on outside issues; hence our name ought never be drawn into public controversy.

11. Our public relations policy is based on attraction rather than promotion; we need always maintain personal anonymity at the level of press, radio, TV and films. We need guard with special care the anonymity of all AA members.

12. Anonymity is the spiritual foundation of all our Traditions, ever reminding us to place principles above personalities.

INTRODUCTION

Just as the Twelve Steps are designed for the personal and spiritual growth of those who are willing to follow the Al-Anon program, the Twelve Traditions are a pattern for the guidance of Al-Anon groups. They are as much a part of our spiritual foundation as the Steps. They describe the purpose of the group and suggest a design that will help it avoid distractions and errors that could dilute or confuse the program.

Consider why some groups flourish and grow, while others, with equally dedicated members, stand still or even fall apart. Most often it depends on how well the members of the group understand and apply the Twelve Traditions.

"Oh," someone protests, "but we're concerned with our personal problems, so we concentrate on the Steps. The Traditions really have nothing to do with improving ourselves." Or, another situation we incur more often perhaps——we hesitate to expect the newcomer to take an interest in anything that doesn't apply directly to a personal problem.

Now that the problem of alcoholism has come out into the open, it attracts widespread attention, from government, the press and from a growing number of professional and less-than-professional counselors. This makes it all the more important for us to preserve the unique character of Al-Anon and the purpose of our groups.

What makes Al-Anon unique is that it is non-commercial and non-professional—and it works. Group membership is limited to those whose lives and peace of mind have been, or are being, affected by an alcoholic, whether still drinking or not.

What are the Traditions for? Why do we need them? The answer for both questions is the same: Al-Anon could never have worked so well for so many without this set of guidelines. The Traditions hold Al-Anon together, working for a common purpose and avoiding whatever might interfere with providing help for every member. They guide us in making decisions which protect the unique character of our fellowship. We turn to the Traditions whenever a problem arises, so we can find the solution that is best for all. They can also be applied to many family and personal situations.

The Traditions are not rules. There are no rules, no "musts" in Al-Anon. Accepting the guidance of the Traditions has been described as "Obedience to the unenforceable." No one in our fellowship has the authority to say "You should not do this," or "You must do that." But if a group fails to observe the Traditions, it risks the possibility of errors and conflict that could deprive many a troubled person of the help to be found in Al-Anon.

All of us, then, can benefit from making ourselves familiar with the Traditions and how to apply them in the groups and in our personal lives. That is why many groups regularly have one Tradition read at the opening of each meeting. Scheduling whole meetings on a Tradition for in-depth study can also be very stimulating.

TRADITION ONE

Our common welfare should come first; personal progress for the greatest number depends upon unity.

This brief statement explained in the Introduction to the Traditions contains the essence of everything in the Traditions which follow. Nearly every point made in one of the Twelve has a definite bearing on the unity upon which we all depend for help in Al-Anon.

Many of us came to Al-Anon to sober up an alcoholic; others came to keep the sober alcoholic happy. Instead, we learned how to face the problems of living, or having lived, with alcoholism and how to correct the way we react to these problems. In fact, we learned a better way of life.

Personal progress in this effort depends on the harmonious working-together of all the group members. Working together requires a willingness to listen to the ideas of others with an open mind, sharing our views with them, accepting what the group's majority has agreed on and not insisting that our views be accepted. Each of us has, however, a responsibility to express those views.

It also means sharing with the others our experience, knowledge and inspiration. It means being willing to take on duties to serve the group and the fellowship—as chairman, secretary, Group Representative, cleaner-up-er, or in any other service role.

Our meetings are made up of talking and listening. Both are essential, but an extreme of either one can deprive others of help. When we have something to share, we share it, but when members use up limited meeting time to go on and on about personal grievances, they aren't helping anyone, not even themselves. True, we all have an urgent need to unburden ourselves when troubles are weighing on our hearts and minds, but that can be reserved for one-to-one talks, when the interchange is more likely to be helpful to both. That's the reason for sponsors, too!

On the other hand, a member who has benefited from Al-Anon experience could try to withhold it at a meeting either out of shyness or a courteous wish to "let others talk." Those who habitually retreat into silence, in this way, may deprive others of something they urgently need to hear. Also, something that is said aloud could open the door to new, personal understanding. The strength of the Al-Anon program comes from recognition of our mutual needs and when we discuss them openly, we help ourselves and others.

An important element in our unity is the use of Conference-Approved Literature (CAL) in our group work. The Al-Anon message and the way it is delivered in our books and booklets is unique. What we read in them has been approved by the members of the World Service Conference, which represents the membership worldwide. Our literature tells it the Al-Anon way, neither diluted nor distorted by a different point of view, as these ideas might be presented in other spiritual or scientific writings.

It is essential for all of us, but especially important for newcomers, to "keep it simple" by concentrating on Al-Anon ideas as they are presented in our Conference-Approved Literature.

Thinking It Over

Tradition One, and the way it backs up the Introduction to the Traditions, can open my eyes to one thing: since I really depend on Al-Anon to make life better for me, I will try to do everything I can to keep the group working for all of us as a unit.

Our common welfare and unity depend upon my willingness to agree with what is best for the whole. This means, among other things, accepting the suggestions of the Traditions on such matters as outside therapies and organizations, our determination to live within the financial means the members provide, concentrating on the program as explained in the Twelve Steps and in our Conference-Approved Literature, and carefully preserving anonymity.

It is common need that brings us to Al-Anon in the first place; like others, I need to find ways to deal with problems related to the alcoholism of a family member or friend. I continue to go to Al-Anon to seek relief from pain and to find a new way of life as a part of a greater whole.

All this can best be achieved where there is free and tolerant exchange of views and where all members understand how the Traditions serve to keep us united in purpose.

I can identify with those who wrote: "Unity of Al-Anon the world over, and the unity of our group, provides us with a core of stability we can depend on. When we are confused and upset, it is a good feeling to know we can rely on our group to give us comfort and reassurance. Later on, we share the responsibility of safe-guarding the group's welfare so it will be there when others need it."[1]

---

[1]*The Forum*, Al-Anon Family Group Headquarters, Inc., Virginia Beach, VA.

A Tradition-One Story

Maybe my experience, painful as it was, will help somebody else to overcome a big handicap—in the Al-Anon program as well as in life.

I have been a member of my group for five years. I have received a lot of help, but somehow I was never comfortable in the group. I stayed because there was no other one nearby. Despite my five years, I never felt I was accepted; there was always dissension about one thing or another, and I was always, I thought, the victim.

About a year ago, we got a new member. She'd had some years in Al-Anon but had recently moved to our town. She and I seemed to click and we became friends. I told her about my difficulties with the group; I had an idea she sympathized with my complaints about the others. One day, on an impulse I can't explain, I asked her to be my sponsor. What an inspiration that was! Imagine a longtime member like me needing a sponsor!

Some time later, when we were having a heart-to-heart talk over lunch, she looked at me seriously and said: "Do you think you could take a shock?" "From you, anything!" I said cheerfully. And she let me have it!

"Well, now, I've come to the conclusion, after long thought, that it's you who are creating the uneasiness in the group. Maybe you don't realize how strong-willed you are; I surely wouldn't have brought this up if I didn't love you." She went on, "I've wondered whether you'd ever taken your Fourth Step with any-one." I said I hadn't so we went into that.

Then she explained very carefully what she thought about the First Tradition, the importance of unity and how one stubborn person could upset it. She reminded me how I'd contradicted others when they were speaking, how I'd argue when somebody reminded me that we were not to bring in non-Al-Anon booklets. She even reminded me of an occasion when I'd told a newcomer what to think.

And I had to admit it all!

You might think this would have brought out anger and defensiveness, but with my Higher Power standing by me, my whole feeling was an overwhelming gratitude for this courageous help from my friend. She must have sensed that I was really ready.

I put my natural determination to constructive use, to continue to go to meetings and to learn to see myself as others saw me. I was ashamed and embarrassed, but finally happy to have that door opened for me.

Once I was able to remind myself I wasn't an all-wise authority on everything, I realized how much damage I had done to the unity of our group and to myself. Now I feel comfortable at meetings, accepting others, as well as being accepted.

TRADITION TWO

For our group purpose there is but one authority—a loving God as He may express Himself in our group conscience. Our leaders are but trusted servants; they do not govern.

Many groups have found themselves in predicaments because Tradition Two was not fully understood and observed. In Al-Anon, there is no such thing as individual authority. All group decisions are arrived at through a majority agreement, reached after all elements of a problem have been considered. We call this agreement the "group conscience."

Our leaders are those who are willing to be servants, those who devote their time, work and love to the fellowship. They have dedicated themselves to serving, not directing or controlling.

The chairman, secretary, other workers in the group, those who serve at the Area Assembly, the Delegates to the World Service Conference as well as the Trustees, the committees and employees at the World Service Office—all these leaders, are "but trusted servants." But such service does not give anyone authority over others. All do their best to serve, relying on guidance from their Higher Power.

When a member has been appointed or elected to a specific office, it is simply an opportunity to serve and to carry out the responsibilities of that job. It is wise for the group to set time limits for each span of service; such rotation will not only share the work of the group, but provides valuable experience to those who serve.

Some members may have an inherent tendency to dominate everyone around them, carrying this behavior into the Al-Anon group. Unless this tendency is self-checked through growth in Al-Anon, the group may find itself controlled by one individual. If this happens, the group has the ability to change this situation and to preserve the spirit of equality through the use of Tradition Two.

Often members of a group are only too willing to let their chairmen and secretaries hold office indefinitely. As long as "George" is willing to do the work, they let him do it, especially if no one is anxious to volunteer. He may gradually come to feel indispensable and important, and, without realizing it, take a managing attitude. We hear of instances in which one member after another leaves because of such group management. Some simply join other groups, but some may have given up on Al-Anon altogether, with no hope of finding the help they could have had in our program.

The work of the group should be shared, and if the terms of service for each job are set in advance, it not only provides other members with the opportunity to serve, but also to gain the experience such service gives.

Another source of difficulty can arise with sponsorship. It is important to make clear the distinction between guidance and advice. Guidance comes through sharing, listening, explaining the program, and pointing out choices available. Guidance never imposes a decision on someone else or dictates a course of action. The use of this Tradition will prevent a sponsor from assuming authority over the member being sponsored; it offers protection to them both.

Al-Anon is a fellowship of equals; we are equally important, no matter what may be our social station, education, intellectual qualities, color, nationality, or religion. Al-Anon's door is open to anyone who really wants to learn how to live with problems caused by, or aggravated by alcoholism in a relative, or a friend.

The comfortable feeling that we are all equals encourages us to take an active part in the work of our fellowship, always with the purpose of serving and helping, never of controlling anyone else.

This idea relates directly to the central theme of all our Steps and Traditions: humility. In Step Three, for example, this humility is described as our willingness to "turn our will and our lives over to the care of God as we understood him."

The progress of the members can be endangered when someone forgets that there is but "one authority" and that authority is not an individual member, nor even a clique which considers itself special. No one speaks for God; it is a loving God as He may express Himself to each of us who forms our group conscience.

Thinking It Over

It is an interesting paradox that those Al-Anon members who have studied our program in depth, and practice it most faithfully in their daily lives, are the "trusted servants" who have come to realize the spiritual essence of Tradition Two.

Using this principle helps the group when an occasional member knows all the answers and tries to control the group or make independent decisions for it. Such a person may be motivated by good intentions, but behind it there is always the thought: "I know what's best." When an individual member assumes such authority, he or she prevents the others from the participation that is so vital to everyone's growth.

Our equality and our uniqueness as human beings are dependent

on realizing that the only authority is a loving God who expresses
Himself in our group conscience.

Tradition Two has an important message for me; practicing it,
not only in my group but in my daily life, will help me on my way
to confidence and serenity.

A Tradition-Two Story

Recently I attended an Al-Anon convention. On Saturday night,
a group of us were having coffee with one of the convention
speakers. Some of us were old friends, some new, but anyone
would have felt at home, recognizing the laughter and sharing.

The conversation was general, until a member of my home
group asked if I had attended any of the meetings in a neighboring
town.

"Yes, I have," I answered, "and I'm never going to that group
again."

"What happened?" asked someone.

"Well, I've gone there quite often and I used to enjoy it a lot. It
was really a great meeting but the last few months it's changed.
Most of the members also belong to AA. All they talk about is
using the program to keep from drinking. I can get that at open
AA Meetings. There's just nothing there for me anymore; I don't
have a drinking problem, and I'm not going back."

One or two other nodded in agreement; they had had the same
experience.

Quietly, the convention speaker said, "I know I'm not from
around here and I don't want to interfere, but do you think you
could go back just once more?"

My rather blunt reply was, "Why?"

"Well," she said, "it seems to me it's really concerned with the Traditions. I'm not sure, I think it's the Second. The members you're talking about must have come to Al-Anon for very different reasons than you're describing. After all, they were already active members of AA. There's a good chance they are unaware it has turned into a 'semi' AA meeting. Some of them may even be disappointed in Al-Anon without exactly knowing why. There's no reason you have to continue going to a meeting where you are uncomfortable, but if you don't tell that group why you are not going to attend anymore, are you being responsible? Aren't individuals who speak, even when they are in the minority, part of what group conscience is all about? Isn't that really how group conscience is formed?

Someone else at the table interjected, "You've been in Al-Anon quite awhile, you know something is not quite right and that there are other meetings, but what about the newcomer? Suppose that it's someone's first meeting and they get the impression that the Al-Anon program is about ways to stop drinking? They may imagine that is great, or they may never go to another meeting, anywhere ever again.

"I'll go with you," said a member who was also a member of AA. "Now I realize why I haven't gone back there; at first, I thought that Al-Anon had nothing different for me, but don't misunderstand. AA gives me the gift of sobriety; I am first and foremost an AA member, but Al-Anon has given me the serenity to accept our daughter's drinking problem."

I thought for a minute and said, "Maybe nothing will change, but it is worth a try—and I used to think the Traditions were dull. We'll go back next Thursday. Wish us luck!"

TRADITION THREE

The relatives of alcoholics, when gathered together for mutual aid, may call themselves an Al-Anon Family Group, provided that, as a group, they have no other affiliation. The only requirement for membership is that there be a problem of alcoholism in a relative or friend.

This Tradition defines precisely what Al-Anon is, and who is eligible to belong to an Al-Anon group. Yet, its purpose and its limitations are not always understood.

It rarely happens that an Al-Anon group, its total membership, allows itself to be drawn into other affiliations. Considering the broader sense of this Tradition, however, we realize that there are, indeed, many pressures and influences on our groups, even from individual members, to involve our membership in other causes, therapies, religions, philosophies or organizations.

After our many years of struggle from small beginnings, we are now recognized worldwide as a dependable source of help. Al-Anon has become a ready-made audience for those who would find it convenient, or profitable, to use our groups for other forms of therapy.

Groups are frequently asked to invite speakers who may, in fact, be specialists in one helping profession or another, but who may not be familiar with the Al-Anon approach to the problem of alcoholism. This Tradition helps us to guard against the confusion that results when we allow our program to be diluted.

Many of our groups have been invited to join others in outside activities or retreats. Some retreats are associated with specific religions while Al-Anon is for people of many faiths, or of none. At Al-Anon, spiritual discussions differ greatly from references to certain dogmas or creeds, which can lead to members feeling out-of-place. The phrase, "no other affiliation," is one of the most important in all twelve of our Traditions. It tells us it is vital to devote ourselves to the study and practice of the philosophy that has proved its power to help people with problems such as ours.

It does not limit, in any way, what we choose to do as individuals, what organizations we might join, where else we may go to seek help in solving our problems or searching for spiritual comfort.

This Tradition says: "the ONLY requirement for membership is that there be a problem of alcoholism in a relative or friend." This simply means that anyone who fits that description may go to any Al-Anon group. Even if a group was formed with the intention of dealing with the special problems of one category of persons, its meetings are open to anyone who is eligible to belong to Al-Anon. This would include AA members whose lives are adversely affected by someone else's drinking. It is up to each individual to make the judgment regarding the circumstances of one's personal situation and need; hence, each person must decide for himself if he needs Al-Anon.

By keeping the Al-Anon program in focus, we provide the mutual aid that is unique to Al-Anon.

Thinking It Over

To me, there is something wonderfully reassuring about this Third Tradition. Although it is directed to the group, between the lines it tells me to fix my mind on the program that can change my life for the better, if I refuse to allow distractions to confuse me.

Tradition Three explains two ways in which my Al-Anon friends and I can "keep it simple." One, is to avoid being diverted from our program by others, and two, is to welcome into Al-Anon anyone who is suffering from the effects of another's alcoholism. Both are perfectly clear. They give me an answer to those who think it would help if the group were to concentrate on problems which are not related to alcoholism, or mistakenly feel a newcomer should be rejected when, actually, he or she does meet the condition for membership.

A Tradition-Three Story

Al-Anon in our city was in serious trouble. It upset me terribly and a confused newcomer was nearly destroyed as well.

I moved here two years ago from another state where I had been active in Al-Anon. At one of the first meetings I went to, I was told that my husband could never become sober unless he first attended a specific treatment center. My husband, however, was sober and had been in AA, at that time, for nearly two and a half years. The Al-Anons also spoke of how sick they all were and said it would take five years to get better. I felt fine, sane and normal after two years of supportive Al-Anon. I have never seen a time-limit for sanity and serenity in any Al-Anon literature. They also told me they thought I was a "co-alcoholic," whatever that was supposed to mean.

At another meeting I told a girl how I felt about myself, and my husband, prior to Al-Anon. Before I could explain that I no longer felt that way, I was told that I needed to go to family therapy at the same treatment center. I told her I was finding my answers in Al-Anon.

At other meetings, I kept hearing terminology and phrases that were common to the treatment program but foreign to Al-Anon. In one instance, a newcomer was told that the only way to detach was to get a separation or a divorce.

We seemed to have two factions: the ones who wanted to adhere to the Traditions and keep Al-Anon—Al-Anon; and the ones who were turning the Al-Anon meetings into an extension of a treatment therapy which I felt lacked the compassion, love and spirituality upon which Al-Anon is based.

Our answering service often received calls from irate spouses who wanted to know why we had advised divorce. We were being confused with the treatment center but, understandably so, since their philosophy had been expounded at meetings.

As for the newcomer I mentioned, she was told at such a meeting that she, as well as her husband, had a progressive disease and, she was either going to go crazy or DIE! She was given a choice: either she and her three children were to enter therapy, which they could not afford, or she should commit herself to a mental hospital. The poor girl was devastated. When she called me, she planned to have herself committed. I talked to her three times that day and once the next morning. Then, I took her to one of the few remaining meetings in the area I knew to be solid Al-Anon.

Things worked out well for this girl, but I wonder how many others there are just like her who don't know anyone to call.

TRADITION FOUR

Each group should be autonomous, except in matters affecting another group or Al-Anon or AA as a whole.

This Tradition gives our groups freedom—complete freedom in all essential matters. Every group is free to choose its own meeting program and topics for discussion; to decide when and where it shall meet; when it will have open meetings, and who will speak at them; and how its funds will be apportioned. This freedom, however, also carries a responsibility for preserving the unity of Al-Anon throughout the world.

Every group and every member is trusted to protect and preserve the character of our fellowship. The Traditions themselves provide our guidance; a group which keeps itself familiar with them is not likely to make decisions which would damage any part of the fellowship. The group is also taking responsibility for presenting a favorable picture of Al-Anon to the world at large, making Al-Anon all the more appealing to those who still suffer and need our help.

Now let's consider some of the happenings that could not be justified by group autonomy:

Sometimes, someone will happen on an idea whose novelty seems so appealing that its creator forgets we're all part of a united fellowship. From time to time, members have decided to rewrite the Twelve Steps and have distributed them to local groups, causing great misunderstanding and confusion.

At some meetings, members have introduced literature which
has not been Conference-Approved but which they felt was superior to our own. In the early days of our fellowship, when there
was little or no literature available, it was helpful to have some
groups voluntarily produce some small leaflets which were sent
wherever they were needed. But with the growth of Al-Anon, it
has become important to have the message consistent in keeping
with the principles of the program.

In the early 1960's, the World Service Conference agreed that
all Al-Anon literature should be Conference-Approved. One by
one, the early productions dropped out, and our literature is now
published only by the World Service Office, with every piece submitted to the Conference for its approval. If any other segment of
the Al-Anon fellowship issues literature that has not been Conference-Approved, it is clearly damaging to the unity of the fellowship as a whole. A unified message in our literature is the glue that
holds Al-Anon together.

On the other hand, it is clearly within group autonomy, for instance, to decide how to open and close its meetings. Some groups
start with a moment of silence followed by the Serenity Prayer.
Others, include the Preamble, or Suggested Welcome. Many read
the Steps, or Traditions, or both. There is just as much variety in
the way meetings are ended. Some use the Suggested Closing,
along with the Lord's Prayer, and others close with the Serenity
Prayer. The choices are many and wide.

Any autonomous action of the group, however, is measured by
its effect on another group, or Al-Anon, or AA, as a whole.

Thinking It Over

This Tradition has made it easy for me to see that every decision we make could be tested by the question: Is this good for our fellowship? Sometimes, groups have ideas that they feel could put our message across to more people who need it. But they have the responsibility to make sure it might not have consequences it would be more prudent to avoid.

A Tradition-Four Story

Just as we were finishing dinner, the phone rang. When I answered, it turned out to be a call from the fourth person who was very unhappy about what had happened in a group in our District.

It seemed that, for three weeks in a row, outside speakers had been invited to address the meeting. One had outlined his method for treating alcoholics in a newly-opened counseling office; at another, a couple explained how they worked with couples; a third meeting was taken up by a woman who told about family therapy at the agency where she was employed.

Each person who phoned was understandably very upset. Some had attended all of the meetings, some only one, but each had gone expecting it to be Al-Anon and had been disappointed. The opportunity for shared experience, strength and hope had been lost. There was no way to undo what had happened.

While it was clearly within the group's prerogative to make program decisions, this was an instance where it also affected the fellowship as a whole. Not only had they needed a meeting and been disappointed, but what about the members from other groups who attended those nights? Or, the newcomer expecting to be introduced to Al-Anon, and finding instead what seemed to be a showcase for professional therapies?

Since I could appreciate their concern, it was doubly hard for me to tell everyone who phoned, that because I did not belong to this group, there was nothing I could do. On the other hand, there was a great deal that each of them could do to insure that something such as this wouldn't happen again.

First of all, they could, as individuals, express their feelings to the group's steering committee and to the whole group. They could become more active and participate in decisions about future meeting topics. Further, they could suggest that group experience had shown it was better to have outside speakers, films, etc., at other than regular meeting times. And, finally, they could point out that more concern be given in planning open meetings.

I was sure that the group members would realize autonomy also carried the responsibility to follow our program, but if the group itself did not see the need to change, I suggested taking the problem to the District or the Assembly. After hanging up the phone, I murmured the Serenity Prayer and went back to the dishes.

TRADITION FIVE

Each Al-Anon Family Group has but one purpose: to help families of alcoholics. We do this by practicing the Twelve Steps of AA ourselves, by encouraging and understanding our alcoholic relatives, and by welcoming and giving comfort to families of alcoholics.

As many of us have learned from applying the Twelve Steps to our lives, the spiritual basis of the Al-Anon program is universal. These Steps, which we borrowed from AA and adapted to our special needs, are being used in similar ways by other self-help organizations—those concerned with gambling, drug addiction, overeating, schizophrenia and other problems.

People sometimes ask why someone who is trying to cope with another's addiction to drugs, or gambling, shouldn't be allowed to belong to Al-Anon. Why do we limit ourselves to alcoholism, they wonder, when alcohol is a drug, and gambling a compulsion? The ultimate success of Al-Anon and its members depends on limiting ourselves to the one purpose: helping the families and friends of alcoholics. Anybody can use our program, but membership is open only to those whose lives have been affected by another's drinking.

Tradition Five suggests that we will best be able to help others, when we ourselves, practice the Twelve Steps. They give us the guidance we need for sharing with each other, by giving comfort and, above all, by learning to listen. For each of us, it is a relief to be able to talk freely to someone who understands.

Helping the families of alcoholics also means guarding against anything that might defeat this purpose. Gossip, for example. Suppose someone tells us about personal family matters; do we remember to be careful not to repeat anything that is told to us? Does the person we are sponsoring, or the newcomer, feel they can safely bring us their secrets in moments of crisis, when they so desperately need someone to talk to and trust?

Giving comfort means we can share our experiences, we can listen, offer our friendship, and allow newcomers to learn to help themselves.

It may be easier for us to see ways of helping "families of alcoholics" than to accept the idea of "encouraging and understanding our alcoholic relatives."

Before Al-Anon, the alcoholic had been the target of all our bitterness and anger. It was the drinker, we thought, who was to blame for everything that went wrong in the family. It may never have occurred to us that this troublesome human being would need, or deserve our compassion. Thus, we are challenged by this Tradition: learning about the disease of alcoholism, and encouraging this person's recovery will work toward our recovery.

What does this say to us who are willing to try to meet the three challenges in this Tradition? It says that Al-Anon is a loving program. By showing concern for other people, we can free ourselves from bitterness, resentment and the anguish of repeated defeat. Understanding and accepting alcoholism as a disease can give us compassion for the alcoholic's suffering and can help bring about our own serenity and spiritual growth.

Tradition Five is made up of ideas so constructive and helpful that it can make a difference in one's life.

Thinking It Over

Tradition Five seems to have three special messages for me. Those messages concern "giving comfort" to people in trouble. I can use the Steps to gain spiritual and emotional comfort for myself; I can gain understanding of the disease of alcoholism and cooperate in the alcoholic's recovery; and I can help others like myself.

Much of my progress in the program is due to learning to welcome every opportunity to respond to someone in need of understanding, comfort and patient, uncritical listening.

When I have times of loneliness, even forlornness, I long for such comfort. I can provide a willing ear and a kind word.

All that's needed is less concentration on my problems, and once I begin to reap the rewards, working this Tradition will be easier and more satisfying as time goes on.

A Tradition-Five Story

Some years ago our group had a new member, who not only needed the spiritual help that Al-Anon can give, but was in obvious need of financial assistance.

She was young, had five small children and a husband who because of his alcoholism was unable to provide for adequate food, clothing and shelter. One night she came to the meeting in tears. There was no food in the house and the children had not had milk for three days. At the time the group had about $60 in the treasury and I suggested that we give $30 of the group's funds to show our love and concern for the young member.

We were about to do this when a more experienced member explained Tradition Five in saying, "our one purpose is to help the families of alcoholics," which means that the group should not offer financial help. Attempts to do this could divert the group from our primary spiritual goals. We decided not to use the group's funds.

In this particular instance, after the meeting a few members, who were in a position to do so, offered individual assistance. One member, who had similar experiences in the past, explained how the young mother might be able to obtain help from a local social service agency.

The wisdom of the group's decision has been made clearer in my growing experience in Al-Anon. Over the years, many members, old and new, have had serious personal financial difficulties. Had we tried to meet these problems with group money, we would have failed miserably, but we did provide spiritual support that made it possible for them to survive. This Tradition does not limit us, but channels our efforts to the areas where we can be effective.

We cannot make alcoholics sober, but we can help the families of alcoholics retain their sanity and ability to function. We cannot meet financial needs, but we can provide the comfort mentioned in Tradition Five when we realize that our strength, hope and experience can be shared, and our own spiritual needs can be fulfilled as long as we do not try again to do things that will divert us from our primary spiritual aim.

TRADITION SIX

Our Al-Anon Family Groups ought never endorse, finance or lend our name to any outside enterprise, lest problems of money, property and prestige divert us from our primary spiritual aim. Although a separate entity, we should always cooperate with Alcoholics Anonymous.

A crucial phrase in the Sixth Tradition is "never endorse, finance or lend our name to any outside enterprise." This concept has always been important to preserve our integrity, but all the more so today because of the growing tendency for people in other organizations to use Al-Anon to advertise or promote their theories and therapies.

The Al-Anon name and our program are designed to help a particular group of people. As individuals we may support, financially or otherwise, any other activity—religious, political, academic, charitable, or whatever else our interests suggest. We may have much in common with other causes, but to endorse or support them as a group could lead to misunderstanding and confusion.

Halfway houses for abused spouses might appeal to many of us as a project worthy of support, but for the group to become involved in the management of such an enterprise would certainly involve it in matters contrary to our purpose.

This is also the reason that, where a clubhouse is established, any member can serve on its board as an individual but it should not be a group project. If a group becomes concerned with ownership of property, large or small, it could leave little time for concentration on our program, thereby diverting "us from our primary spiritual aim."

In keeping with this Tradition, Al-Anon does not endorse films or literature produced by other organizations, no matter how good they may be. This Tradition also speaks of cooperation with Alcoholics Anonymous. This does not mean giving financial support, or forming combined Alcoholics Anonymous and Al-Anon groups. To serve its membership, a group must either be Al-Anon or AA; it cannot be both. On the other hand, some Al-Anon groups periodically plan joint open meetings with an AA group; and an occasional talk by an AA member at an open Al-Anon meeting can be interesting and helpful. If invited to speak at an AA meeting, Al-Anon members tell their own stories, not the alcoholic's, and emphasize how Al-Anon has helped their recovery.

There are many ways for us to cooperate with AA that help us both achieve our "primary spiritual aim." When both fellowships participate in a convention, there are suggested procedures to assure cooperation. Large conventions require considerable advance planning, and those interested in having the other fellowship participate can begin by inviting a liaison member to attend planning sessions. Each fellowship should be responsible for its own agenda, speakers and activities, while the host would be responsible for the overall plans, renting the facility, etc.

Another area in which Al-Anon and AA may cooperate is where Al-Anon has not grown sufficiently to support its own Al-Anon Information Service Office or Intergroup. It may share facilities with AA when offered, provided that Al-Anon meets its portion of the financial expenses (desk space, telephone, etc.) and the responsibility for handling all Al-Anon Twelve-Step calls. When

Al-Anon grows strong enough to support its own office, separate facilities from AA are desirable.

Thinking It Over

I think this Tradition is most important in protecting Al-Anon's identity and preserving its unity. I can resist the desire to solve all the world's problems, the temptation to get my Al-Anon group's support for any number of worthwhile projects, for I have learned the hard way that diversions cause disunity and controversy.

More and more, I hear of groups where other versions of "what to do about the alcoholic" are discussed, and where our members, adding one or more such ideas to our meetings, divert us from the practice of a program which works. I can keep my enthusiasm for these causes but not refer to them in my Al-Anon meetings. The study and practice of our Steps and Traditions is the way to serenity.

How grateful I am to AA for the principles of this program, but I also realize that our separateness is our mutual strength.

A Tradition-Six Story

One of my responsibilities in the World Service Office involved answering several weekly inquiries requesting names of films made by outside agencies which could be shown at Al-Anon events. The staff answered these inquiries based on the circumstances. In some instances, it seemed helpful to show a film which conformed to our philosophy, at an open meeting or a convention. However, it seemed inappropriate to show the same film at a closed meeting where people go to concentrate on the Al-Anon program for personal recovery.

The situation became more and more uncertain since there were no specific guidelines to which we could refer. Both volunteers and staff at WSO shared the dilemma; so many films had been made recently that accurately reflected the Al-Anon philosophy. Since we reached no conclusion, we brought this question to the attention of the Policy Committee. Recognizing the serious nature of the problem, the Policy Committee Chairman appointed a special committee to study the issue in depth. A questionnaire was sent to all World Service Conference Delegates asking just how films were used in their Areas in the hope this would reveal our best direction. We learned there was extensive use of outside films at every level of Al-Anon service, and wide support for the maintenance of a list of films "approved" by the World Service Office. With this guidance, the Policy Committee submitted a recommendation to the 1978 World Service Conference that such a list be maintained.

In the lengthy discussion of this proposal at the Conference, Tradition Six came alive for me. I couldn't help but be impressed by the frank, unheated exchange of views; it was truly an example of open-mindedness and group conscience at work. We even viewed some of the films at a Conference session and found them to be beautiful; but the majority listened when a few Conference members pointed out that approval would constitute endorsement of an outside enterprise. The proposal was defeated almost unanimously.

I had seen the Tradition work for the protection and unity of the fellowship worldwide.

TRADITION SEVEN

Every group ought to be fully self-supporting, declining outside contributions.

Our financial pattern is simplicity itself, yet questions do sometimes arise that need to be clarified.

According to Tradition Six, money contributed to a group by its members is not to be used for "outside enterprises." This money is for Al-Anon purposes alone.

Here in Tradition Seven, we see the other side of the coin: where a group's money comes from. As already indicated, the main source is the contributions the members drop into the basket when it is passed at each meeting. There are no dues or fees but, as part of a greater whole, each group takes responsibility for supporting local, national and worldwide Al-Anon services. Each group is free to decide how much it can afford to contribute to each of these activities. Most of our groups are willing to provide what is needed, since every Al-Anon member shares in the benefits of this support.

Contributions by members at their regular meetings are usually adequate for all Al-Anon needs. For those who have a surplus, there is always an opportunity to carry the message by buying literature for distribution to institutions, churches, schools, doctors' offices and elsewhere. Occasionally, however, a group will have a need to raise extra money and will hold a white elephant sale, or a raffle.

In keeping with this Tradition, the membership supports the World Service Office by means of contributions by the groups, individual members, donations from Area Conventions and the sale of Conference-Approved literature. When groups support the work of their service arms, the members can expect them to be responsible to the groups' needs. This mutual interdependence is a wholesome and sustaining condition preserving all Al-Anon in unity and equality.

The last part of the Seventh Tradition refers to "declining outside contributions." The groups, as well as the World Service Office (our key to worldwide unity), are subject to this Tradition. If group support were inadequate, the WSO would be tempted to accept outside donations, which would change the entire structure of the Al-Anon fellowship and destroy its basic spiritual concept.

In the past, many offers of financial support have been received from non-members who thought we were doing something worthwhile. Was it ungracious not to accept these donations? No, because we realized such offers could carry expectations with them. If accepted, we might feel obliged to make concessions to the donors. Even in a small way, it would mean selling a bit of our independence. To keep Al-Anon free of outside influence, we must look to ourselves for support.

Thinking It Over

In the simplest terms, this Tradition points out one of the cornerstones of the Al-Anon program of recovery. When individual members and individual groups understand that they are responsible for their own survival and progress, a great spiritual strength flows into each part as well as the whole. If I do my part and others do theirs, we do it together, and we don't need to ask someone else to do it for us.

A Tradition-Seven Story

Our local Information Service recently received a letter from the director of a nearby facility for the rehabilitation of alcoholics, with a check enclosed. The letter read in part:

"We decided to contribute $150 toward your superb work. Many of our staff have become acquainted with the Al-Anon Family Groups during their work here. We have both admiration and appreciation for the help you are rendering to the families of alcoholics. May the best of God's blessings continue to be yours as you invest your time and talents in the healing of others."

That gracious gift would certainly have been difficult to refuse but for our Tradition Seven. How easy to fall into the trap of evaluating agencies, or of favoring one facility over another, because we felt indebted to it. Our answer, in part:

"Thank you very much for your interest in the Al-Anon Family Groups. While we are most grateful for your generosity, we cannot accept the check you sent because Al-Anon is self-supporting according to its Traditions. We are delighted to hear that many of you have found Al-Anon useful and we hope you will continue to suggest how valuable our program can be to families who are suffering."

TRADITION EIGHT

Al-Anon Twelfth-Step work should remain forever nonprofessional, but our service centers may employ special workers.

An integral part of Al-Anon is Twelfth Step work, with each member helping others in need of comfort and a new approach to living. The reward of such work is the joy of sharing what we have found in this fellowship. There is nothing professional in any of this; what we do for others is not done for money or any other material gain but to further our own spiritual growth.

Al-Anon's service to so many troubled people around the world is our major responsibility. In the groups, no matter how many or how large they became through the years, Al-Anon service has remained non-professional. The major purpose, for everybody, is to foster an opportunity for a loving interchange of help and encouragement through personal contact. So it is today, with more than 28,000 groups of people in many lands, speaking many languages, embracing many different faiths.

Tradition Eight provides guidance to the members who happen to be professionals (counselor, clergy, physician, social worker). Their exchanges in meetings should be on a member-to-member basis with their own recovery as their primary concern. They do not attend Al-Anon meetings in their professional capacity or as experts in the field of alcoholism.

The second part of Tradition Eight says "our service centers may employ special workers." When Al-Anon was new and set up the original "Clearing House," the office chores, letterwriting,

119

record-keeping and housecleaning, were done by volunteers; but, as we grew, we needed full-time people for the ever-growing tasks of this central office. Experienced workers had to be hired and paid (however little!) for the work they did.

Today, the business affairs of the World Service Office, in so large and far-reaching a fellowship as ours, require business organization, not only to assure orderly procedures and maximum production, but to fulfill the requirements of state and federal laws. Workers with various skills are needed: accountants, secretaries, editors, and many other specially-trained people, who are not necessarily Al-Anon members. The World Service Office Staff Administrators, trained in a particular phase of service (Alateen, Institutions, etc.), are, however, always Al-Anon members.

Service centers throughout the world may also employ special workers. They, too, follow the precepts of the Twelve Concepts explained in our Service Manual.

Thinking It Over

As time goes on, the Eighth Tradition takes on more and more serious meaning for me. Some of our members have taken extensive training to become professional counselors; others may project the jargon and method of the counseling they have received; sometimes professionals join Al-Anon because of their personal needs. For this reason, it is often difficult for me to keep the line sharply drawn between professionalism and Al-Anon. The Eighth Tradition reminds me to keep Al-Anon free of alteration or dilution.

Once again I discover a basic principle of our program. We have no authority figures. To recover, we meet as equals and help one an-

other, not because some are experts and others are learners, but because we all have needs and strengths.

Our group has found that an occasional meeting on this Tradition is helpful to avoid confusion on this point.

I keep repeating to myself, "Let's keep it simple; let's keep it Al-Anon."

A Tradition-Eight Story

In growing up, and in my chosen career, my life had always revolved around professionals. How could nonprofessionals ever supply help to me? That seemed impossible, but that was before Al-Anon. It wasn't until I had some personal experience in testing out this Tradition that I realized its validity. Perhaps its truth lay most importantly, not in the harm that I did to Al-Anon, but that I hindered my own recovery. I tried to mix professionalism into my own program; it didn't work.

When I first had contact with the program, I latched onto it, I thought, as the answer to all my problems. Here was a place where the difficulties of the alcoholic family were really understood. What I realized was that all those wonderful people had experienced the same suffering and could empathize with the pain. No one gave advice; there were only suggestions from the experiences of individuals who had used the tools of the program and found that they worked.

As I began to feel better, I wanted to help others too. With all the years of postgraduate schooling and training I had had, I felt well qualified! Why did it never occur to me that I hadn't even been able to help myself with all that training?

When I started helping people, I was flooded with phone calls from other Al-Anon members, most of which must have sounded more like consultations than Twelfth Step calls. Although many members seemed grateful for my help and benefited from it, something began to happen to me. I lost the program. I had become a "professional" and I went downhill—badly. I became depressed and hopeless. I had stopped using the program for my own recovery.

It was not until I had reached a bottom lower than any I thought possible, that I made a telephone call in desperation, a call to help myself. A dear, loving, understanding member gently suggested that I come back to the program—for me.

Since then, many good things have happened. I am a professional, working in the field of alcoholism. I owe a great deal of my success to my own recovery in Al-Anon, recovery which must continue as a member of the fellowship. When I go to meetings, I go to get help for myself, and to share my feelings and growth with others. The Al-Anon program pervades every area of my life. While at work, I suggest participation in Al-Anon to families and friends of alcoholics, but I do not expound on the program. I go to Al-Anon meetings as a member of the fellowship, not as a professional. I can be *A Pebble in the Pond*, * and I have learned when not to throw a stone.

*The title of Public Information booklet, (P-42).

TRADITION NINE

Our groups, as such, ought never be organized; but we may create service boards or committees directly responsible to those they serve.

In an organization, people at various levels have the authority to direct the activity of others. A fellowship of equals, such as ours, doesn't work that way. In an Al-Anon group, no one may give orders or expect obedience of anyone. We get our necessary work done by the use of spiritual principles and logical procedures agreed upon by everyone involved.

True, a group does elect, or appoint, individual members to take care of various chores: a program chairman, secretary, treasurer, Group Representative or any other necessary group officer. These trusted servants are responsible to perform faithfully the jobs they have accepted. It is they who help provide refreshments or pay rent for the meeting place; group funds are used for both, of course. According to the wishes of the group, and in line with our Traditions, they invite speakers, plan meetings, lead meetings, keep members informed of matters of interest, take care of finances and dispense them. Officers are rotated on a regular basis; no one stays long in any position so that all have a chance to share responsibility.

These individuals are given an opportunity to serve the group and the fellowship. This does not include a right to direct, or control the other members.

123

While the groups only require minimal structure, our "service arms" must be sufficiently organized to work effectively. The "service boards or committees" mentioned in Tradition Nine include the following: Information Services, central offices of an Area, its Assembly, and the World Service Office (WSO), which is the clearinghouse for all the Al-Anon Family Groups. These service arms have committees or boards which deal with specific areas of the overall work and may also have salaried employees who carry on the day-to-day functions. They have no authority over the groups they serve. Instead, the members, who have become knowledgeable in a specific phase of service, have a responsibility to listen and respond to the voice of the fellowship.

Thinking It Over

Through the years my understanding of the meaning of this Tradition has grown. At first, it seemed to me that a group had to have qualified leadership and rigid structure to avoid chaos. Later, I mistakenly felt the Tradition meant that no officers were needed. Now I realize that certain jobs must be filled to give form to the meeting. Rotation of office guarantees that all have a chance to grow through service.

I know I am in Al-Anon for my own recovery, and by volunteering to serve on the necessary committees, I translate phrases such as, "I am responsible" and "Let It Begin With Me" into action.

A Tradition-Nine Story

A letter to the World Service Office outlined a group problem, a problem that has occurred over the years in one form or another in other groups:

"The five members who started our group two years ago consider themselves to be the 'Charter members.' They have drawn up a set of rules and regulations which they say we must follow. They enforce a no-smoking ban, call the roll at each meeting, record minutes and also close the business meeting to everyone they don't consider to be members of our group. They even have a sign that says 'KEEP OUT.

"We have a lot of disharmony and, at present, the 'Charter members' are deciding who they will ask to leave the group. One member has been told she cannot attend because work makes her arrive late. Can the WSO help us?"

The answer from the WSO read in part:

"Tradition nine cautions us about groups being organized. First of all the term 'Charter member' is not used in Al-Anon. People who form groups very quickly turn over leadership to newer people so they, too, will have an opportunity to serve and grow.

"Business meetings are conducted in several ways. Some groups hold a business meeting during their regular meeting; others hold one before, or after the regular meeting so that program time is not taken up with business. A number of groups prefer having a steering committee which is usally made up of the present officers. This is not a decision-making body. Its function is to suggest matters to all the members so that a vote can be taken. This is how a group conscience decision is reached.

"Maybe the group might consider reading the Traditions before their meeting and might be interested in taking a group inventory."

TRADITION TEN

The Al-Anon Family Groups have no opinion on outside issues; hence our name ought never be drawn into public controversy.

Tradition Ten goes further than Tradition Six in confirming, once more, the purpose of all our Traditions—to keep ourselves, as a group and a fellowship, clear of anything not related to our program.

Those of us who are deeply concerned with other causes may be tempted to share them with the group, by bringing them up in group discussions or as topics for talks. But, within the fellowship, the one thing that has brought us together must remain our sole concern. If we fail in this, it could lead to controversy, not only within the group, but on the public level.

Tradition Ten suggests that Al-Anon should not take a stand for or against public issues such as child abuse, segregation, politics, or any current social causes, however important they may be to members as individuals. Such involvement could lead Al-Anon into public controversy which might seriously affect our unity and continued growth.

We are a fellowship of many thousands; our members are of many races, religions, and nationalities and have a wide variety of viewpoints. Taking a position on any outside issue would surely divide us from within. A free, unbiased, uncontroversial atmosphere in which to develop belongs to all. Individual Al-Anon members carrying the message at the public level do not express opinions on outside issues; Al-Anon, as a fellowship, has none.

Suppose an Al-Anon group were to become actively involved in a worthy outside project, even one that may seem akin to our common bond, such as supporting legislation for funding rehabilitation of alcoholics. Even if we were able to have all the members of the group agree, there might well be another Al-Anon Family Group with differing views and solutions. Given any worthy cause, each approach to the problem may be different and result in division. Supporting any outside cause diverts us from our primary spiritual aim. And then, if we pursue one worthy cause, why not pursue others?

While Tradition Ten refers specifically to controversy on outside issues, many members feel the spirit of this Tradition makes controversy of any kind an unwelcome guest at Al-Anon meetings. Members coming from hostile atmospheres that often prevail at home may well be discouraged by controversy at meetings. Each of us, wounded by the effects of this disease in our lives, comes to the Al-Anon meeting seeking comfort and understanding, free from dissension. We are free to disagree with one another, but we try to do so without angry disputes.

By avoiding rancor and controversy, Al-Anon members of differing political and ideological beliefs have been able to come together at meetings and share their experiences in dealing with alcoholism in an atmosphere of mutual respect. In Al-Anon, we can concentrate on our common bond and not on our opposite views on outside issues.

Thinking It Over

The emphasis in this Tradition is on our avoiding anything that would lead to public controversy.

How often I am tempted in a meeting to speak out against some social or political evil or to encourage others to declare their opinions. Instead, I try to concentrate on the Al-Anon program.

I am responsible, personally, to do my part in insuring that Al-Anon not become involved in any question that could focus public attention on my group as part of some political, social or religious cause. Such activities are time-consuming; they distract us from our primary purpose.

Tradition Ten reminds me again of Al-Anon's reason for existing: to help families and friends of alcoholics. As a service to myself, to my friends in the fellowship, as an Al-Anon member and to Al-Anon as a whole, I will avoid anything that would link the Al-Anon name with any public question.

A Tradition-Ten Story

Some years ago, a series of articles appeared in a local paper in our state. The author attacked the not-for-profit status of Al-Anon and accused the fellowship of soliciting funds from the general public and not accounting for their use. The author went further, demanding an investigation of Al-Anon by the State Attorney General.

Quite a few of our local members sent copies of the articles to the World Service Office suggesting that it was the responsibility of the office to refute these "bald-faced" lies in a letter to the editor.

While it was a natural reaction for the members to want to respond, Tradition Ten kept Al-Anon from becoming involved in a public controversy. Neither the author, nor the paper, was contacted directly by the World Service Office, but pertinent records were supplied to the Attorney General at his request. The documentation made it apparent that the charges were false and the Al-Anon name was cleared without having to offer a public denial.

TRADITION ELEVEN

Our public relations policy is based on attraction rather than promotion; we need always maintain personal anonymity at the level of press, radio, TV and films. We need guard with special care the anonymity of all AA members.

When Tradition Eleven was drafted, the words "public relations" had a broader connotation. In more recent years, this term has been associated with commercial, profit-making, or fund-raising organizations. The motivation of such organizations is different from Al-Anon's. For this reason, we now use the more definitive term "public information" in our literature to describe our efforts to let people know about Al-Anon. We're not promoting, but rather trying to attract and comfort those whose unhappiness and confusion we understand so well. We want others to know that friendship and help are waiting for them in an Al-Anon group.

Over the years, the media has increasingly recognized Al-Anon and its work, and this recognition has brought many newcomers into Al-Anon. Often a single unsolicited mention by media representatives has brought inquiries from thousands of people in search of help.

Giving information about our fellowship has been an important part of our job from the earliest days. In a sense, every one of us is a medium of public information, but in spreading the message, discretion must be our watchword. The Tradition specifies, too, that anonymity be maintained when we appear in public. We re-

131

main anonymous in publications, film, radio or television to keep personality build-up in check. Since we are all equal in Al-Anon, no individual stands out as an important representative of the fellowship. This is a direct confirmation of the theme of our Steps— humility. If members parade their association with Al-Anon and build a personal following, it gives a distorted picture of the nature of our fellowship.

On the other hand, there are members who misinterpret this Tradition and keep their association with Al-Anon so secret that they never use an opportunity to share its help with someone in need. Members doing Public Information service or acting in a specific office, such as Area Delegate, give up a certain measure of their personal anonymity, since they are the contacts with outside agencies as well as within the fellowship. This is still within the Eleventh Tradition, since it does not break anonymity at the public level of the media.

The last sentence of Tradition Eleven refers to the anonymity of all AA members. It suggests that, in all situations, we do not reveal the full name of anyone in AA.

In the final analysis, it is a matter of judgment. We want everyone to know about Al-Anon's availability. We do this best when we are careful not to distort our program by trying to sell it or by making promises we cannot keep.

Thinking It Over

This Tradition has a very special message for me. It reminds me that the emphasis of our Twelve Steps is on humility. In stressing personal anonymity, this Tradition is saying I am no more important than anyone else in our fellowship, so I won't be tempted to stand

*forth as a representative of Al-Anon. I can best attract by the power
of example. On the other hand, I don't have to keep my identity a
secret if I plan to have others contact me.*

*While the Tradition places the emphasis on anonymity at the pub-
lic level in the media, it is also a gentle reminder to me not to feel that
I have been especially devoted to the fellowship in service. Each one
of us does what we can to be helpful to other members, but service
and loving interchange are their own rewards and need no praise or
applause. Service makes us all equals.*

A Tradition-Eleven Story

I was chairman of an Al-Anon Intergroup in the capital city of a
large country, where Al-Anon had been trying for some years to
develop a workable structure to unify the widely scattered existing
groups. One day, we were approached by a national TV station to
tape an interview about our program. It was a wonderful opportunity to carry the message. Three other members and myself partic-
ipated in the taping, in the course of which we appeared full face
to camera and proudly gave our full names, also explaining that
our husbands were all AA members. They had given their permis-
sion for this disclosure.

The same evening, the Intergroup was hosting a large meeting
in honor of several Al-Anon members who had come from another country to share their experiences with us. Immediately after
I had announced at the meeting that this taping was soon to be
broadcast, one of our visitors pointed out that to divulge complete
names with full face to camera and identify ourselves as Al-Anon
members and wives of AA members, was contrary to the spirit of
the Eleventh Tradition. It could prove most damaging to the

healthy growth of Al-Anon in the future by distorting the basic principle of anonymity, the cornerstone of our fellowship.

Fortunately, it was possible to contact the TV station the following day and they agreed to withhold the tape and do another interview in which we appeared as Al-Anon members, using first names only and with back to camera. The program was subsequently broadcast nationally and brought many new members into the fellowship, reassuring them that their anonymity would not be endangered.

TRADITION TWELVE

Anonymity is the spiritual foundation of all our Traditions, ever reminding us to place principles above personalities.

In Al-Anon, one of our greatest gifts is the privilege of helping others find their way out of darkness into light. We help others, and keep ourselves open to being helped. There is no room in this important purpose for self-glorification and pride, and much room for gratitude, humility and willingness to serve.

The same theme runs through our Steps as well, beginning with the word "powerless" in the First Step. The power we have comes from a Higher Power and not from our own wisdom and virtue. This is directly stated when we are reminded to place principles above personalities.

The Twelfth Tradition reaffirms the principles of all our Traditions. When we act and think as a member of Al-Anon, we are able once more to see that our will alone does not determine the reality of a situation.

When we subordinate our will to the spiritual strength of the group, unity adds to the healing process. When we do not emphasize our uniqueness, we gain strength from being part of a group conscience which flows from a power greater than ours alone. When we leave our other affiliations outside Al-Anon's doors and recognize the common problem that brings us together, we often feel for the first time in our lives that we are where we belong.

Through this sense of belonging, when we stop holding ourselves aloof, comes a realization that the material values that ruled our lives before Al-Anon, are no longer important. We are responsible for our own recovery and measure it in spiritual terms.

Principles are everything. Accepting this idea may not be easy since it requires true humility. Eventually we realize, with a sense of discovery, that this Tradition has within it the basis for change that can lead to solutions of personal, family and group problems. Our spiritual growth through humility has its roots in the principle of anonymity.

Thinking It Over

Placing principles above personalities, as Tradition Twelve suggests, presents a paradox. Throughout my study of the program, I am reminded to be aware of what I am doing, how I am reacting to others, what I can do to improve myself and my life. This surely means thinking of myself a great deal. Won't this make me self-centered? Won't it keep me from caring about other people and their needs? Not if I remember the principles I am asked to follow in Al-Anon, and use them as a yardstick in what I do and how I relate to others. Tradition Twelve tells me principles are more important than I am, for I still have a long way to go in striving to fulfill my role in life.

A Tradition-Twelve Story

Since attending Al-Anon, there are several lessons I have learned which come to mind when I think of anonymity and the spiritual idea behind "principles above personalities."

The first lesson occurred during my early Al-Anon days. When I look back, during that time my attitude was one of many curious contradictions. There I was, full of fears and insecurities; yet, at the same time, I was such a snob. I sat at meetings in judgement of others. I decided that certain members who made a good appearance and seemed intelligent had something to offer. Others, I concluded, couldn't possibly have anything of interest to say to me. It's ironic, but one of the people I disregarded because of poor grammar was later to become my sponsor.

My next difficulty with Tradition Twelve came about because I placed the trust, that should have been reserved for my Higher Power, in other people. Completely defeated by alcoholism, I gave the alcoholic such control over my life that I had no other Higher Power. Next, I transferred this dependency to other Al-Anon members. These were several well-spoken members with winning personalities that I admired. When they said something was so, I took it as gospel truth. How shattered I was when I learned that some of my idols had feet of clay, and how unfair it was for me to put them on a pedestal. I had to learn the only one who deserved that kind of blind trust of faith was my Higher Power.

My third lesson, and one that I still struggle with, is not to allow my personal knowledge about a member to interfere with what they say. For example, there was a member of my group who had wonderful words of wisdom about detachment that I needed to hear. Knowing her personally, I took her inventory and unfortunately concluded, "Why should I listen to her? She's not doing such a great job with her own detachment." When I recognized my distorted thinking, I asked myself, "Who am I to judge how another person works the program?" Today I try to remember the words my sponsor passed on to me, "Don't discount the message just because you don't like the messenger."

The way I see it now, what happens within a group transcends the individual. As I observe this spiritual principle of anonymity, the more willing I am to learn from everyone, the more able I am to decide what is appropriate for me.

EPILOGUE

Al-Anon Around the World

The unending flow of letters to and from members all over the world—from many nations, many religions, in many languages—proves that, in Al-Anon, we are one, united by a single, simple, spiritual program.

A letter from one member sums up beautifully the way the program works. It said in part:

"I often think of a picture that came to my mind when I first read the Twelfth Step and tried to understand it. I looked back on my troubled life, before Al-Anon, when I felt as though I were groping around in a terrifying black cave. There was no way out. No matter how desperately I prayed and struggled, I was trapped. There was no way out of the hopeless confusion of my life.

"Suddenly someone, a stranger, took me by the hand and led me around a turn in the cave that opened up into a tunnel, dotted by a row of lights. He led me as far as the first light and said, 'Just keep following the lights and you'll be all right.' I didn't care where they led just as long as I could get out of the black despair I was living in.

"As I walked from one light to the next, the path through the tunnel became more and more bright and my fears gradually faded. Finally there came the brightest light of all—sunshine and freedom!

"The lights were our Twelve Steps and our Twelve Traditions which kept showing me the way out of my confusion. With them I felt wholly secure.

"I knew there were many others like me who couldn't find their way to that tunnel lighted with the lamps of hope. Remembering my own pain, I tried to start many others to that ultimate sunshine we find in our beautiful program."

THE TWELVE CONCEPTS

The Twelve Steps and Traditions are guides for personal growth and group unity. The Twelve Concepts are guides for service. They show how Twelfth Step work can be done on a broad scale and how members of a World Service Office can relate to each other and to the groups, through a World Service Conference, to spread Al-Anon's message worldwide.

1. The ultimate responsibility and authority for Al-Anon world services belongs to the Al-Anon groups.
2. The Al-Anon Family Groups have delegated complete administrative and operational authority to their Conference and its service arms.
3. The Right of Decision makes effective leadership possible.
4. Participation is the key to harmony.
5. The Rights of Appeal and Petition protect minorities and assure that they be heard.
6. The Conference acknowledges the primary administrative responsibility of the Trustees.
7. The Trustees have legal rights while rights of the Conference are traditional.
8. The Board of Trustees delegates full authority for routine management of the Al-Anon Headquarters to its Executive Committees.

9. Good personal leadership at all service levels is a necessity. In the field of world service, the Board of Trustees assumes the primary leadership.

10. Service responsibility is balanced by carefully defined service authority and double-headed management is avoided.

11. The World Service Office is composed of standing committees, executives and staff members.

12. The spiritual foundation for Al-Anon's world services is contained in the General Warranties of the Conference, Article 12 of the Charter.

GENERAL WARRANTIES

In all its proceedings the World Service Conference of Al-Anon shall observe the spirit of the Traditions:

1. *that only sufficient operating funds, including an ample reserve, be its prudent financial principle;*

2. *that no Conference member shall be placed in unqualified authority over other members;*

3. *that all decisions be reached by discussion, vote, and whenever possible, by unanimity;*

4. *that no Conference action ever be personally punitive or an incitement to public controversy;*

5. *that though the Conference serves Al-Anon, it shall never perform any act of government, and that, like the fellowship of Al-Anon Family Groups which it serves, it shall always remain democratic in thought and action.*

INDEX

A

AA *see* Alcoholics Anonymous

Acceptance 5, 8, 13, 21-22, 25, 28, 34, 37, 39-40, 51, 59, 64, 71-73, 76, 87, 90-91, 97, 136

Admitting
admitting powerlessness 7-11 First Step
admitting wrongs 31-37 Fifth Step, 63-68 Tenth Step

Affiliations 99-102 Third Tradition, 135

Al-Anon 97, 99-102 Third Tradition, 120-121, 141
as a fellowship *ix, xi-xii*, 76, 86-87, 93-94, 103-106 Fourth Tradition, 111-114 Sixth Tradition, 115-117 Seventh Tradition, 119-122 Eighth Tradition, 123-125 Ninth Tradition, 127-130 Tenth Tradition, 131-134 Eleventh Tradition
as a way of life *ix-x*, 9, 33, 63, 87, 89
history *xi-xii*
meetings *xi-xii*, 8, 55, 76, 78, 80, 86, 91, 103-104, 110, 113, 115, 119, 122-125, 128, 137
closed meetings 113-114
open meetings 112-113
program *ix, xi*, 13, 78, 80, 85, 88, 94-97, 101, 107, 112-114, 120-122, 127, 139
purpose *ix-x*, 85-86, 89, 93, 107-111, 115, 129, 135
separate entity 111-114 Sixth Tradition
see also Affiliations, Authority, Autonomy, Concepts, Cooperating with AA, Leaders, Membership requirement, Name, Principles, Public Relations, Steps, Traditions, Unity

Alateen 62, 120
history *xi-xii*

Alcohol 7-11 First Step

144

146

148